DEDICATED
to
John and Cynthia Wright, friends of my youth,
who are growing old along with me.

CONTENTS

Poem: As I Grow Old 9
Introduction by Wayne E. Oates 11

Author's Preface 15
Physical Stamina 19
Friends and Neighbors 39
Money 61
Recreation 85
Educational Opportunities 109
A Healthy Mind 133
Spiritual Strength 159

Epilogue: Top of the Mountain 181
The Author 183

AS I GROW OLD

God keep my heart attuned to laughter
    When youth is done;
When all the days are gray days, coming after
    The warmth, the sun.
Ah! keep me then from bitterness, from grieving,
    When life seems cold;
God keep me always loving and believing
    As I grow old.

                           — *Author Unknown*

INTRODUCTION

Although I rarely read books line for line, I found myself reading this book almost word for word. Glenn Asquith speaks as an older person *with* older persons. He does not take a hortatory approach. He creates in his reader a sense of being conversed with, of having been listened to carefully by the author before the lines he is reading were written. This book is one of the few internal-frame-of-reference treatments of the issues of living creatively as an older person. It is written from *within* the world of the older person himself or herself.

Approximately one in ten Americans is 65 years of age or older. In 1900, by contrast, only one in 25 persons was above the age of 65. It is estimated that by the year 2000 there will be at least 28 million persons 65 and over in the United States.

These persons are not only becoming more numerous; they are becoming more articulate. They challenge all sorts of myths on what it's like to be an older person. A recent Harris survey found that 61 percent of the 18-64 age group thought loneliness was a serious problem of older people. Only 12 percent of those 65 and older reported viewing loneliness as a serious problem. Whereas 50 percent of the younger group saw poor health and fear of crime as serious problems for the aging, only 23 percent of those above 65 perceive these to be problems. Whereas many people are sure that persons above 65 would prefer to be with people their own age, 74 percent of older persons themselves indicate they prefer to be with people of all ages. Yet, the same survey shows that the most bitterness among older persons involves the issue of mandatory retirement. Among those who have retired, a substantial 37 percent said they did not stop working by choice — they were forced to retire. [1]

All of these realities are given flesh and blood in the witness and testimony, guidance and wisdom of Glenn Asquith in the pages of this book. The author takes the conclusion of a physician that "there is nothing good about growing old" as his theme. He agrees that some things are not so good. But he maintains that some aspects of aging are good. He transcends the wisdom of the doctor by pointing out that the best can be made of both the things that are good and the things that are not good. He approaches the issues of aging from seven different perspectives: (1) the physical, (2) the social, (3) the financial, (4) the recreational, (5) the educational, (6) the psychological, and (7) the spiritual.

These are *aspects* but not separate divisions of the totality of the older person's life. As Asquith writes about each aspect, the reader gains a distant awareness of the relevance of that aspect of life to the totality of life. One benefits from the perspective of a man who sees life steady and sees it whole, a view of life very much akin to

---

[1]. American Association of Retired Persons, *News Bulletin*, November 1974.

the wisdom and integrity with which Erik Erikson characterizes the ideal life of the older person.

The special contribution of this book is the empathy which it creates for the inner world view of the older person as a person. One senses that the older person is like everyone else, with the added advantage of the wisdom of the years. The reader does not get the feeling that older persons are a breed apart, a separate subspecies of the human race. To the contrary, regardless of the age of the reader, the author communicates a kinship with his reader. This provides a rare vitality for the book.

The refreshing new angles of vision for the aging are subtly evident in a sort of offhand way. For example, the view of recreation as a reward for years of service well done is rarely thought of by many. The thought of formal education as a pursuit that calls for different and qualitatively higher motivation in an older person who is free of success drives and competitive needs was new and refreshing to me. I found something on page after page that will be useful in understanding motivation for living at any age, not just during the mature years.

The author's competency for this work is an earned one, since he has already written several books in other fields of learning and experience. He approaches the task autobiographically but does not put himself at the center of his writing. A reader senses that Asquith is "there" and is "with" what he is saying but does not feel that Asquith is writing some sort of "swan song" or "story of my life." To the contrary, Asquith finds in himself the universals that are in people of all ages, and only especially in the aged.

I commend Dr. Asquith as an accomplished writer whose lucid insights on aging and the aged make his reader look forward to the next book from his pen.

Wayne E. Oates
Professor of Psychiatry and Behavioral Sciences
University of Louisville School of Medicine
Louisville, Kentucky

AUTHOR'S PREFACE

My doctor said to me, "Mr. Asquith, there is nothing good about getting old."

At the age of sixty-six I found this statement somewhat terrifying. I was among those from whom the physician had taken all possibility for further good!

And I realized that this doctor was speaking from long experience and observation. For many years he had watched his patients deteriorate by the aging process. He had walked often through the corridors of nursing homes. He had ministered to hundreds of men and women in the geriatric wards of hospitals. As I thought of this background against which the doctor placed his conclusion, I was reluctantly inclined to agree with him. But, before bowing to my fate, I decided to test the truth of his statement, "There is nothing good about getting old," against the situations of other periods of life.

Thinking of youth as the opposite of age must I say, then, "There is nothing *bad* about being young"? Nothing bad? But what about the restricting disciplines of home and school, the desolation of broken friendships, the disappointments of losing in sports and games, the agony of adolescence, the forlornness of breaking off a first love? No doubt youth is glorious in its physical ease and in its dreams and joys, but there is much that is bad about it.

Skipping to middle life, can we say, "There is nothing *bad* about being in the prime of our years"? What a surge of satisfaction to be doing well at a chosen job, to acquire a home and establish a family, to be among those who to some extent are the movers and shakers of the world, to feel the deliciousness of the appetites of the mind and body with the abilities to satisfy them and the strength to enjoy the satisfying! But there are also the worries of family life, the fear of losing the job, the struggle to make ends meet financially, the shadow of insecurity cast by world conditions, the jealousies and rivalries of personal and career efforts. Despite its triumphs, middle life has much that is bad about it.

If other periods of life have both good and bad, must we accept the premise that maturity and old age have *nothing* to offer? Is it not possible that getting old will disclose the same proportion of good and bad that we found earlier in life? Is it too optimistic to agree with the poet, Walt Whitman:

> Youth, large, lusty, loving — Youth full of grace, force, fascination!
> Do you know that Old Age may come after you, with equal grace, force, fascination? [1]

I determined to look into all of this, and I did, and I have put down my findings in this book.
Glenn H. Asquith
Cherry Hill, New Jersey

---

1. Walt Whitman, "Youth, Day, Old Age and Night," in *Leaves of Grass*.

PHYSICAL STAMINA

We would be foolish to insist that our physical condition has nothing to do with our feeling, our thinking, and our willing. Sometimes we speak of "surroundings" and "atmosphere." We find that we perform best when the room in which we work is decorated and furnished to our taste in a way that is consistent with our standards and ideals. Much of the crime and degradation and drug addiction among the poor can be traced back to the horrible environment in which they must live day after day. To a degree, the same forces influence us when our "body house" falls below our desires and demands.

There is a difference, however. The self can rise above physical deterioration to a greater extent than people can rise above a slum location and a shabby house. We cannot hope to move out of our body to better ourselves and must make the best of what we have! The poet Waller had a happy thought about this:

> ... the soul's dark cottage
> battered and decayed,
> Lets in new light through
> chinks Time has made.

First, what can be good about this physical reckoning?

The Good

By the time we approach retirement age, we have learned by experience that *the body is durable and resilient*. Many years ago a medical authority wrote an article on the ills that attack the human body. He ended on the encouraging note, "You are tougher than you think." Looking back, we are appalled at how many weary miles we have propelled this body along sidewalks and streets and at the endless stairs we have climbed. We recall, with some horror the tons of food we have eaten, and the thousands of gallons of liquid we have drunk. Through all this the body has proved durable. Suppose we had been given the privilege of shopping for a body that would wear well, that would not shrink, that would remain in style through the years. How could we have done better than select the body that is ours? It has been a tough body, and the toughness has not gone out of it as much as one might think.

And what of resilience? We have subjected the body to extreme temperatures. We have called upon it to do without rest or sleep for long periods of time. We have contracted and expanded it in our work and play. We have changed its normal processes by drugs and X-rays. We have exposed it

Physical Stamina

to blows and bangs and falls. But this body has bounced back every time. Like a rubber band that is stretched, the body has come back to size and shape and normal functioning when the tension has been relaxed. This splendid quality of resilience is still in our body despite the ravages of the years.

Since our past experience with our body testifies to its durability and resilience, we can have the assurance that it will stand many more bouts with the events of life.

A second fine thing about the body is that it has *learned to live with certain aches and pains*. When a twinge appears here or there and announces itself, we do not panic. We know what the discomfort is. We've experienced it many times before and it has been diagnosed as harmless. In fact, our regular aches and pains are like the old friends whom we have known for years. These friends have annoying traits and habits, but they are our tried and true companions. We would not exchange them for unpredictable strangers.

This knowledge of aches and pains comes slowly. When we were young we were impatient with any discomfort of the body. We considered it as abnormal and needing correction. We sought out doctors for prescriptions and regimens that would rid us of all pain. But now we know that parts of the body have their small imperfections which they indicate by growling a bit.

The physical has its moods as well as the emotions and these fluctuations must be allowed. In fact, the body is almost a seasonable organism with summer, fall, winter, and spring complaints.

The parade of aches and pains comes at expected times of the day and year. Although we do not welcome the pains, we know that they are as reliable as the first robin and, honestly, wouldn't we miss them?

Aches and pains are respected as proofs of life. Many of us remember the experience of coming out of anesthesia following an operation. Waking up, we began to see articles in the room, and faces. Soon we felt the pain from the surgeon's work. The pain assured us that we were still among the living. We had survived the operation.

Even though we are getting old, the body is alert and sensitive. We can depend on it to register any new pain that will serve as a warning. The old aches and pains make up a sort of test pattern. The body runs through its complicated computer system all intruders that might be dangerous to us.

A third good thing about our body as we grow older is its *second wind*. Athletes often report that after running or playing to the point of exhaustion they suddenly experience a new surge of energy and are able to go on. In a sense, this is true with us who are getting older. This mature period of life is the second wind of earlier days.

Like a pitcher in a crucial ball game, with the score tied and the bases loaded, we are able to reach back and come up with something extra. Life has taught us the magnificence of our physical stamina. In the emergencies and tight places when we need a little extra, we find that it is there. The years have given us the key to this storehouse that is often hidden in younger years.

Physical Stamina

Two new pastors of churches in New York started their work with great energy and success, but soon the Christmas season came upon them with its great demands and expectations. Both of the ministers became exhausted and were physically unable to preach the Christmas Sunday sermon. The two churches had to call back the pastors who had just retired because of age, and they responded and carried the day with ease and splendid results. These older men had the second wind.

People often say, "You don't know what you can do until you try." And this is true. We who are getting older have tried many times, and we *know* what we can do.

Often we are given the opportunity for demonstrating this second wind. Sometimes we may be called back, as were the preachers, to fill in somewhere in our old capacity — in office, store, factory, schoolroom, kitchen, or nursery — and find we are able to deliver a better performance than when we were bearing the burden and heat of the day. How can this be explained? How else than that age has given us a grace of the second wind? Freed from our old occupations we may well find that we can branch out into new pursuits with vim.

A fourth good thing about getting old physically is that we have learned the value of a day. *Every day we are privileged to live becomes a bonus.* A popular actor who had reached the age of seventy-six told an audience that when he wakes up each morning he turns to his wife and says, "Well, we have made it again, old girl!" No longer do we assess our life ahead in the vague terms of years and decades. We are aware, suddenly, of what a marvelous thing each day is. We know that we are never given more than a day at a time in any case. We cherish our day and extract from it every bit of its sweetness and joy. To express this feeling within myself I wrote this bit of verse:

> Old people cannot sleep;
> In the morning they rattle things
> And disturb their married children,
> And their grandchildren
> Who ask, in drowsy petulance.
> > "Why must you get up so early?"
>
> But the older people cannot answer that;
> They do not know.
> They only know the day is dawning,
> One more precious day crammed with sights and sounds and odors,
> One more period of light before darkness;
> Freedom of space to move their arms and legs and lips.
>
> How can the young understand?
> > Their cup of life seems brimming,
> > A few drops wasted — what does it matter?
> But when the nectar is low in the glass and there will be no more
> It must be savored sip by sip.
>
> > Where, then, the marvel that
> > Old people cannot sleep? [1]

---

1. Glenn H. Asquith, *Christian Herald*, April 1961. Reprinted by permission.

If getting older brings with it no other reward than a new appreciation of what a day can be worth, the cost is not so high after all.

The Not So Good

Admittedly, some physical factors are less than desirable in our experience of getting older.

There is the stark *fact of obsolescence*. Obsolescence means to be worn to the point of no further active use, or to be aged beyond current demands. Automobile manufacturers have been accused of deliberately building obsolescence into their cars to assure that the owners will purchase new models at regular intervals. Certainly the principle is true of the human body — except the styles do not change! For more centuries than we know, the human form has been coming off the creation assembly line without annual changes. But the human body does wear out. As we noted earlier, we put many miles on our bodily speedometers and wear and tear are inevitable.

This obsolescence may be dealt with to some extent by our physicians and surgeons. Some parts can be removed for the benefit of the whole. Artificial substitutes are available for worn-out veins and tubes. Organs may be replaced or modified by operation. However, these repairs are not miraculous reversals of the aging process. We must learn to live with the fact of lessening efficiency and get used to squeaks and rattles here and there.

Happily, we do not wear out in every place at once. Our teeth may give us trouble first, or maybe our eyes or ears. Our decreasing sense of balance may slow us up somewhat. Our stomach may require some discipline in eating and drinking. Our legs may be stiffer and weaker and not so ready for the nonchalant journeys of younger days. Parts of our body that we were scarcely aware of before now issue strident cries for attention.

We may look at this obsolescence in the way that a housewife looks at her home. Does she want it to be painfully neat, almost sterile, with everything always in its place? Or does she prefer to have a warm "lived in" atmosphere? As far as the body is concerned, we cannot make the choice. Physically we have that "lived in" look whether or not we prefer it. But isn't that the way most of us have preferred our homes? A home is for joyous living and so is the body. And living brings worn spots to the body just as it does to rugs and furniture. But the living is worth the price.

Continuing with the not-so-good, we find that this obsolescence of our body expresses itself in a *change in our functions and senses*.

If our ears are affected, we may at first complain that others do not speak clearly. They do not enunciate as they should. They whisper too much! The change in the sense of hearing is hard to admit, but it is a common ailment and certainly no disgrace. Sometimes a hearing aid will help. Sometimes greater concentration during a conversation will be of value, Sometimes instruction in lip-reading will be a partial answer.

If our eyes are affected, glasses must be worn, and the prescription changed regularly. Sometimes minor or major operations will improve the sight. Magnifying lenses are easily available. The

Physical Stamina

"fine print" in insurance policies, directories, and other places may give us trouble. We may miss some of the visual details of things that once were clear to us. This may force us to think more and read less. This slightly different world need not prove less profitable than the previous state if we learn to adapt ourselves gracefully.

The senses of smelling, touching, and tasting usually are the last to be affected. Or perhaps they are the last to be noticed because they are not so vital to our proper functioning and enjoyment as seeing and hearing. We are aware that these senses are aging when we long for something that tastes as good as a special dish our mother used to cook! Or when the aroma of flowers seems not so sweet as formerly. Or when we brush against something or someone and our "radar" does not warn us as quickly as before. These disabilities rarely come to the point of being a serious problem and may be borne jauntily.

The slowing down of our senses increases our reaction time. Some older drivers try to prove that they are as good as ever by whipping their cars through traffic with abandon and jamming on the brakes suddenly. The driver in front always stops too soon! We can escape being a menace to others if we use more care in our driving and other activities, making allowance for any changes in our alertness and quickness of response. This is not giving in to age, but a sensible acceptance of ourselves as we are and a concern for the safety of ourselves and others.

Another disagreeable truth to be dealt with is that the older body needs to eat more carefully.

The television commercials that assume a person may eat anything he wants and as much as he wants if he takes some kind of pill or liquid afterward are not for us. Without depriving ourselves of the true pleasure of eating, we need to exercise good judgment in the kinds and quantities of food and drink we consume. This will help assure comfortable days and uninterrupted nights.

Before we close this section, we should consider the unpleasant possibility of mental deterioration. We are cheered to read newspaper accounts of people who reach the age of one hundred without losing the keenness of their intellect. These are fortunate, but rare, individuals. Because of the tensions of life that have pressed upon us, our eating habits, our type of occupation, our inherited genes, and disease some of us are susceptible to mental infirmity. Years ago this misfortune was thought to be the inevitable harvest of long years. Now, however, much medical progress has been made and the true causes are being brought to light. Hardening and thickening of the arteries is the most frequent reason for mental slowness and confusion. Medicine and diet can do much to control the problem. As we get older we should consult a medical doctor in whom we have confidence and follow his advice carefully. If we start this in our sixties our chances of keeping reasonably alert mentally are very good.

Another not-so-good warning sign is that our capacity for sustained or sudden *exertion is limited*. The old days when we boasted of being able to work around the clock or stay at a party to "all hours" are behind us. An occasional lapse may not hurt, but as a lifestyle this is no longer appropriate.

One guide is the index of weariness. It is best to stay at a task, or a pleasureable pursuit only until the body begins a polite complaining. The old saying about the wary warrior fits here: "He who fights and runs away will live to fight another day." For example, when we had an automobile trip of 500 miles or so to make when we were younger we were likely to avoid a delaying stop and "drive straight through." Now such a trip should be divided into two or three parts in as many days. A good rule for all our major undertakings might be, "Don't drive straight through."

A cheerful side of this not-so-good limitation of exertion is that it does not necessarily limit the quality of our exertion. For instance, a man who is good at carpentry can no longer stick at a job for eight hours with regularity. But putting in fewer consecutive hours need not lessen the quality or beauty of his product. A woman who used to do all of her shopping in one day need not find that her joy in the buying and her ability to choose wisely and economically are lessened by spreading the activity over several days. It is well to cultivate an image of ourselves as quality people, rather than quantity people.

A final not-so-good aspect of our physical condition is that we perceive as never before that *we are going downhill*. Sometimes a doctor tells his patient that the course of the ailment cannot be reversed but that there will be plateaus on which the downward trend will rest for a while. In a sense, getting old is an incurable thing — we will not say disease — and there can be no backing up. But there will be happy plateaus when we seldom notice any distinct change. These plateaus will be more frequent if we are willing to accept our limitations and take good care of ourselves. There will be months, sometimes years, when we feel the goodness of life afresh and enter a period that a poet spoke of as "A land in which it seemed always afternoon. [2] We cannot get back to midday, much less morning, but we seem not to be going rapidly toward the sunset. As with Joshua, the Old Testament warrior, the sun seems to stand still.

Nevertheless, the long trend is downhill. We are, after all, in the process of completing our life cycle. For every morning there must be an evening and a night or the day could not be complete. In the Old Testament story of Creation the order of the periods is comforting to us who are getting older: "And there was evening and there was morning, one day" (Genesis 1:5). The evening is in a way the precursor of the day and its purpose for being.

Making the Best of It

Since our physical condition is as it is, there is only one way of dealing with the situation — make the best of it. Worry, repining, rebellion can only hasten bodily breakup. Cheerfulness and determination to refuse defeat can keep us in the best possible condition at our time of life.

We might start with the exterior and take a look at how we may *keep our appearance attractive*.

---
2. Alfred, Lord Tennyson, "The Lotos-Eater."

"Hah," we might say, "who would ever notice me or care what I look like?" Unfortunately, people do observe us and rather expect us to become a bit careless. As the years take their toll our hands may tremble when we eat and spots will appear on our clothing. Our aging eyes may not detect spots and wrinkles and lint and empty buttonholes. Some of us may find it most difficult to maintain a uniformly commendable appearance. We must try harder and not permit ourselves to be lost in the anonymity of "old people."

Our selection and care of clothing should concern us. Our budget for wearing apparel is not likely to be large and we must buy with care. But attractive and well-fitting garments are not more expensive than drab and poorly cut garments. We should avoid styles that elicit undue attention and bring criticism from younger folks who may say, "What's that old codger trying to prove?"

Careful choice of the colors we wear will make for attractiveness. Color makes nature beautiful. Nothing clashes. Everything is blended in a natural way to please the eye. Careful choice of basic colors and appropriate contrasts for accent will please the eyes of those who see us in our homes and on the streets.

Neatness is another asset to an attractive appearance. One needs to be quite young to be pleasing to the eye clad in old jeans and a "sloppy Joe" shirt, with hair blowing in the wind! Let's not try it! Neatness communicates our ability to take care of ourselves. The neighbors of a man in his eighties frequently remarked on his neatness. His nails were always clean. He wore gloves for dirty work. When he went away from home he always put on a clean shirt and a tie and made sure his shoes were shined. Many people measure our competence by how we look.

And something that enhances our appearance but cannot be bought in a store is alertness. One of the signs of health in animals detected by veterinarians is alertness. When a cat or dog takes no visible interest in sights or sounds he is marked as an ailing animal. Is not this true of us? How can we present a fairly constant picture of keen interest in all that goes on around us?

One thing against us here is that we have experienced so much in our lifetime. In a television commercial two young people are the guests of an aged man and he is showing them his mementos. In awe they say, "My, you have seen it all!" And the older man replies, "Yes, I've seen it all, I've done it all." Cars on the street, children jumping rope, the seasons of the year, a fire siren, holidays, the song of birds — we have seen them all, we have heard them all so many times. How can we be expected to quiver with excitement when the routine we face is like a parade repeating itself?

If we can conceive of the parade as not being an identical one that keeps going around the same block, but an endless procession with each participant one that we have never seen before, and if we can think of each noise as coming from a new instrument, the seeming similarity may not be so oppressive. To a careful observer of snowflakes, this winter's snow is not just the same as that which fell in the great blizzard of '88. Snow is a treasure of exquisite flakes, each of which is different from all others that have fallen from the beginning of time. In the same way no person, animal, bird, sound, or event coming to our notice today is precisely the same as any other we have come across in our lifetime.

Another step toward making the best of our physical condition is to *make friends of diet and exercise*.

"Diet" is not a popular word. With activities and pleasures fewer as we get older, there is the tendency to give in to appetite. Fat or thin, what does it matter? And we take particular notice of news items that report people living to a ripe old age who have always eaten and drunk whatever they wanted. I knew a woman of ninety-nine whose friends were counting the months hoping she would reach a hundred. When I called at her house one day she was eating chocolates. Several boxes of candy were on her table. Her daughter saw that I was a bit surprised and said, "Oh, the doctor told us to let her eat all she wants. How can she do any harm now?" However, few of us have reached ninety-nine. Common sense tells us to eat in moderation and to avoid food and drink our doctors ask us to avoid. Even if we were fortunate enough to escape a shortening of life by indulgence, what of the quality of life? To feel as well as is possible, to be as vigorous as possible, to be able to do as many things as possible is certainly worth more than a brief indulgence of the taste buds — not to mention the fact that we might well suffer an incapacity which would make us a burden to others.

Diet involves choice of foods, frequency of eating, and quantity. Each of us, with the advice of his physician, may experiment with these three factors — choice, frequency, and quantity — until a wise routine is worked out. The results can be pleasant and need not make meals drab.

"Exercise" is another word that rarely creates enthusiasm among us. Older years bring on the "rocking chair" complex. Tomorrow seems the ideal day to do things that require some effort. But this attitude can bring on a flabbiness that, combined with our aging, will destroy the very comfort that we think we are enjoying by taking it easy.

Good books are available on systematic exercise for older people. Indeed, even people bound to wheelchairs, limited by past illness, or otherwise unable to engage in the usual exercises can benefit from a systematic tensing of muscles. Such exercises are discussed under the term *isometrics*.

For those of us who are able to get out, walking is one of the best exercises to be found. There is an exhilaration about walking that is lacking in more formal exercises. The mind and eye can be occupied with a thousand other things without interrupting a steady walk. And walking can take us to interesting places.

Perhaps we should link diet and walking, for walking must be taken in doses that will not be too much or too little. Here, again, our faithful doctor should be consulted.

If we are sold on walking, we ought to remember that it is an art. Putting one foot in front of the other is not exactly walking at its best. Sauntering is not walking. The speed of walking may start at a slow rate, gradually increase, and then settle down to a brisk gate that will tone up the muscles and encourage deep breathing. When tiredness appears, the walk should decrease in speed until vigor returns. For a person in reasonably good health, five miles a day is an ideal distance to walk — perhaps with half of this distance scheduled for morning and the other half for the afternoon.

A final and perhaps unexpected suggestion for making the best of our physical condition is to *come to terms with the end of getting older — death*. This has a strong bearing on our physical well-being. For instance, if we proceed on the vague presumption that we are going to live forever, we will be so tense and worried about every change that comes with the years that we may make ourselves ill when we need not be. Ignoring the inevitable may actually hasten our end. We need to keep ourselves as clear as possible from all obstacles to good health.

We might go back to what we found about our completing the life cycle. Illustrations of the life cycle are abundant in nature. Deciduous trees, for example, shed their leaves in the fall, remaining bare of limb for months, and then burst forth with buds and new leaves. They repeat this cycle year after year. Grass, flowers, and seasons of the year are additional examples of the cycle. And we are not exceptions to the process, except that a return to vitality after age is not apparent. We cannot see others regain their youth, and we are worried.

Most of us have some belief in a new life, in a new situation and condition beyond death. We must embrace our faith firmly until it becomes a guideline to daily living just as diet and exercise.

Contentment with our ultimate end may come by realizing that the "I" within is too vigorous to be encased in our body "house." The house gets old but not the "I" and we cannot suppress our longings for a better place in which to live. Since the aging process is not reversible, our only escape is by death. Death, then, becomes a work of love upon us by the Author of our existence.

Another way to approach this finality might be to think of the "remittance men" of some generations ago. In England a younger son who could not inherit property or title, or a man who had done something beneath the dignity and honor of his family, was encouraged to live abroad. Regular payments for his living expenses were sent and called "remittances." As long as the man stayed away from home, his money was assured. If he started back to England all funds were cut off. If the man lived long enough, things would change at home by the death of older people or by different attitudes toward the offense, or by time erasing bitter feelings. In this event the man would receive the "last remittance" and be ordered to come home. In this life, we have certain allowances of years and strength. But we can expect a final remittance and the call home.

An acceptance in faith of our own inevitable death is a great necessity for us who are getting older. When our minds are clear and serene about this inescapable culmination we can get down to the business of living with zest. Our general physical state will be improved.

FRIENDS AND NEIGHBORS

Our interaction with other people — the joy and companionship of shared experiences — is affected by aging just as much as other aspects of our lives.

The Good
One good thing about the changes we experience in later years is that now *we have more time for others*. We find increased opportunity for being with a wider circle of neighbors and acquaintances and people involved in community affairs.

Perhaps one of the curses of younger years is the crowded time schedule. No matter how we tried, we could not find more than twenty-four hours in a day, and these had to be portioned out over many fields of activity. Work accounted for about a third of the time; sleep called for another third; personal care, eating, study, the newspapers, shopping, and travel time between appointments made a wreck of the third that was left. Because free time was scarce after we had cared for the "must" things, leisurely gatherings or long visits with others were not too frequent. Now that we are getting older we have some flexibility in the work and the miscellaneous thirds of our day. We finally have more time for one another.

Instead of five minutes we may have fifteen or twenty for a social contact. Rather than a half-hour limit for a call we may have an hour or two. In younger days when we knew that we could spend only so much time doing something, the time seemed short because our mind was intent on the next responsibility. Now we need not think, "The children will be home from school soon. John will be expecting me at six o'clock. Sally is depending on me to take Billy to Scouts. That meeting is called for eight. I must get going. I will miss something." It's amazing how much longer an hour can be when we know that nothing is about to pounce on us to drag us away.

This freedom from, "Hurry, hurry, hurry!" can enhance our relationships with those whose lives we touch. With more time to interact we wonder how we ever missed the good qualities that we now find in men and women and young people who once were only casual acquaintances or complete strangers.

With this added time comes another good thing — *awareness of community*. We may have heard the line, "No man is an island" (John Donne), or we may have read in the New Testament, "None of us lives to himself, and none of us dies to himself" (Romans 14:7). But how many of us have taken the time to explore the deep meaning of commu-

Friends and Neighbors

nity hidden in these expressions? Now we do have time to give thought to our place among others and to our interdependence in community.

We speak of living in a certain community. What does this mean to us? Perhaps that we are grouped in houses or apartments within a certain area, that we shop at the same malls, that we join our taxes with those of others to assure fire and police protection, schools, sewers, and a local government. Together we can provide these necessary and good things; separately it would be impossible to have so many advantages. But are these life-enriching services and facilities community, or are they the result of community?

Even the average dictionary will define "community" as a "body of people." As we grow older we become increasingly aware of this prime characteristic of community. The firemen, policemen, sanitation men, teachers, store-owners, and clerks are people. They are flesh and blood. They all live somewhere not too far from us. And the other taxpayers are people who find it difficult to pay their share, too. Every house or other dwelling unit we pass shelters a family or a person. As we grow older there is time to think about this. The increased opportunity for considering mutual concerns will encourage us to make some human explorations.

We shall realize that by coming to live in a particular community we have accepted responsibilities. A community does not survive of itself. Paying taxes is just a part of what a community member should be doing as his share of the total effort. Opinions should be given on vital issues and votes cast at meetings of the community. Frequent elections demand our participation. Community endeavors that are over and above the tax structure will fail or succeed according to the will and work of community members.

This growing awareness of community will do much to take from our vocabularies the easy word "they" and to replace it with "we." A television advertisement showed a man with a bad cold complaining, "If *they* can send a man to the moon, why can't *they* find a remedy for *my* cold?" Now we begin to realize that we have been depending on other people for much of the good that we have and hope to have in life. If all others in the community sat back and waited on that mysterious group called "they" to act, what horrible kind of community would it become?

As we rejoice in our new awareness of community, we will want to consider how we may participate *in volunteer, community projects*. In the business of our earlier years we may have been vaguely aware that older people were engaged in volunteer work for the public good. We saw them in hospitals in uniforms working in the wards, pushing carts, manning telephones, working the cash register in the gift shop, clerking behind desks. We saw them driving Red Cross cars and replacing books on the shelves in our local library. Now we can join these volunteers by yielding to our urge to be of use and of help.

We might well start with the hospital nearest us. The director of volunteer services will be able to indicate what openings are currently available. Hospitals use both men and women volunteers.

Each hospital, of course, has its particular needs. An effort is made to match the applicant to a job that is appropriate for his strength and skills and the time that he wishes to contribute.

In addition to drivers, the Red Cross may need people to work in blood banks and to be on call for emergencies.

A fairly new organization called Fish needs volunteers to use their own cars to transport infirm people to hospitals and doctors' offices.

The local school system may use older people as teacher's helpers or playground assistants — and sometimes in the cafeteria.

An application to the proper person in the Social Agencies office in the community will disclose other jobs needing to be done and for which no money is provided. Clinics, day nurseries, and other such facilities may appreciate volunteer help.

This list of possibilities is just a beginning. Each community has its own special needs. If we do not find a suitable volunteer activity in our own area, we can check in a nearby city or town.

Volunteer service is one of the good things about getting older because of the satisfaction that comes from doing for others what has been done for us through the years, or what may be done for us later as we become less able to care for ourselves. There is also a fine comradeship in being in the company of those who give themselves to mankind in whatever way opens to them. We now have time to be with people and enjoy them even as we hope to be a source of joy to others.

A final item of good in our changed social life is the chance to *recapture the spirit of shared fun*.

"Fun" is a word that has taken a beating in our time, but it still expresses something of exhilaration. Fun implies a simple enjoyment without any solemn purpose. We associate fun with laughter. Many of the toys given to children today are labeled "educational." Children, supposedly, can have fun learning about tools, household appliances, chemicals, microscopes, and quiz cards. As we get older we need to recapture some pure fun and forget about any profitable outcome.

And the key word is "shared." It is difficult to have fun by oneself. This is where the social self takes over. Solitary enjoyment passes for pleasure, but if we are in the mood for *fun* we need a group of people to join in the merriment. What fun is there if I make a witty remark with no one to hear it and laugh with me? What enjoyment would you have giving a clever impersonation if there were no one to see and hear you? This is the need behind the preference of older people to do things "together." If there is a trip or excursion to be made the fun is multiplied by filling the car or, at least, by going as a foursome. Could we imagine a man playing out his eighteen holes of golf alone? Or a woman who prefers to play Scrabble by herself rather than with friends?

We need other people in all areas of life, but especially to have fun. Fun is built on admiration and response. The child going through his playful antics always says, "Watch me!" And the older boy gets on his bicycle and cries, "Look, Ma, no hands!" The fun for the child requires someone to admire him or laugh with him. As we get older we experience that simple human urge for

Friends and Neighbors

admiration and response. Having some fun in a group helps us feel kinder toward our companions because we see in them qualities that had been hidden before. So enjoy the wonderful release that fun brings. Let it lay the groundwork for a more understanding companionship with others.

The Not So Good

Although we are finding that there are not-go-good features in each area of life as we grow older, the negative aspects related to the social part of life may prove to be the hardest to accept and the most painful to endure. What must be borne alone is bad enough, but what is experienced in company may often be worse.

To begin with, we find that *we are not included in the plans of others* with the regularity we had come to expect. And now this means more to us than when we were younger. Then if we were omitted from some activity we could easily find another — and we had so much to do that we didn't care much either way. But with our outlets for mingling limited by our new circumstances each instance of being shut out can assume major proportions to us.

If we have a family, we notice that the activities of our children and grandchildren are gauged to their age and needs and often not suitable for older people. We may sense that we are a bit in the way when we are included and begin to wonder whether or not we were invited because the family felt it a "duty" to remember us. Older people are often thought of as "sitters" to stay with young children while others go out "on the town."

We may find that our younger friends begin to make up their dinner lists, their party lists, their foursome lists, and their occasional get-togethers without including us. We find ourselves disappearing from the holiday and birthday lists of many whom we thought of as permanent friends. Without any malice on their part they may be omitting us simply because we have dropped from the usual active scenes, or because we have moved and they have mislaid our address.

Our former fellow-workers and business associates may no longer feel the need to invite us to their gatherings since whatever prestige we brought earlier by our presence is now gone. One who can only tell how he used to do things can be a nuisance among people who can say, "This is what we are doing now."

Little by little we find one event after another that we once took for granted closed to us. This exclusion hurts for a while, but we may counter the disappointment with the thought that we must have been guilty (if that is the word) of omitting older people when we were younger. And, after all, the purpose of an older person in life should be different from that of the younger. To get right down to it, would we willingly accept certain invitations even if they were offered? Our tastes are changing. Would we enjoy, for instance, talking shop when we are no longer part of the shop? Age has opened a different door and we might as well go in and see what is offered.

Still, if we have some lingering twinges of disappointment at being shut out, we might go a step further and consider why we no longer move

Friends and Neighbors

in the same circles and with the same status. This reason is that, on the basis of our age, we are considered *out-of-touch*. Let's see if this is true.

If the activity to which we are not invited is a trip to a motion picture or theatrical performance, our family or friends may have selected something that will include words and scenes and expressed ideas that they think could "shock" us because we are not in step with the new boldness of dealing with sex and social problems. It will be thought that we are fastened firmly within the framework of our more Victorian upbringing.

And more than likely, we are considered out-of-touch with the latest in our former field of interest or endeavor. Does the older housewife know much about the new craze for "organic" and "natural" foods? Does she understand the use of the new, complicated sewing machines? Can she keep up with the latest in home decorating and furnishing? Does the older mother know anything about Dr. Spock and the new freedom and permissiveness in families? Does the older teacher see the good in the "open" classroom and "free" schools? Does the retired doctor know about the latest findings in drugs and surgery? What about the latest theology insofar as the older rabbi or minister or priest is concerned? And the older mechanic or laboring man, the older telephone operator or store clerk? What could they do with the labor-saving gadgets and the computers? Older people are considered to be out-of-touch.

This out-of-touchness with which we are saddled extends into changes in modes of thought, standards of behavior, international affairs, modern art expressions, contemporary literature, the generation gap, church changes, and more. In brief, we are thought not to be "with it" any longer. We have had our day and our place in the scheme of things. Now we are expected to sit back and hold fast to antiquated ways and customs and ideals and morals, and to shout our indignation against the younger generation.

How true is this common conception of the aging as being out-of-touch? There is just enough truth in it to disturb many of us.

We find, by searching our souls, that we do prefer older ways of doing things to what we see going on around us. The new methods seem not to turn out the solid product that we think our ways brought forth. But even if we are right in our conclusions this does not excuse us from being knowledgeable about what is going on these days.

Although we may not be able to stem the tide of rejection because of our supposed backwardness, we owe it to ourselves and to our critics to make ourselves aware of all current trends and expressions insofar as our strength and abilities permit. If we care to be a part of our world, we must at least acquaint ourselves with its unfolding developments. A comparison of the older and newer may bring us to the conclusion that we are actually more in touch with reality than some of the younger people who lack the perspective of our years!

Going along with our listing of the not-so-goods we cannot deny the fact that now *we must accept appointments and "dates" with an "if."* Some of our grandparents made a habit of ending their acceptances of engagements with the letters, "D.V." — *Deo volente*. "God willing." We find that now we must end our acceptances or hopes of being in company with letters indicating, "health willing," "weather willing," "finances willing," and the like. As we get older certain considerations may well keep us at home when we would much prefer being elsewhere.

Of course, in our younger days these same considerations frequently kept us from doing things and caused us to disappoint our family and friends. But they occurred less frequently. Now stumbling blocks preventing our going out are more common. We have far less certainty of being able to keep our word when we accept an enticing invitation. This in itself is one of the reasons why we are not included in the plans of others. The thought in the minds of our former associates might well be, "Oh, he (or she) probably wouldn't be able to get out, anyway."

One of the main hindrances to being able to do what we want when we want to do it is health. Some of us may continue to enjoy good health well into old age. Nevertheless, it is wise to avoid undue exposure and fatigue, especially when we have a cold, a bout of arthritis, or a stubborn infection. When we were younger, these things might have been considered minor and we would go our way despite them. But in later years, small things are more likely to grow worse if not treated with respect. The same health problems require different care according to age and vitality.

The same caution extends to weather conditions and other incidental concerns. Whether or not it was wise, in younger years we may have had the swashbuckling attitude, "I'll be there, rain or shine, come hell or high water. Count on me!" And so we exposed ourselves to the elements and came back, probably, none the worse. As we get older we may as well accept the fact that we are not as resilient as we were and think carefully about the relative advantage of missing some event or risking ill-health. Such denial on the one hand may reward us with the health to enjoy several other social opportunities.

Another not-so-good social change as we get older is that we are *either hemmed in by contemporaries or suffer a dearth of them* An older person needs contemporaries with whom to share reminiscences and doubts and from whom to take courage. Only contemporaries can understand our particular problems and our particular joys.

We may find ourselves hemmed in by comtemporaries in a retirement "village" or apartment complex operated exclusively for older people. These places offer much by way of security. Usually there are restrictions about admitting strangers. Often a daily room or house check makes sure everything is in order. The availability of an infirmary may be part of the arrangement. This all helps provide a warm feeling of being cared for without any real loss of independence. However, because these developments are for older people only, companionship with others of varying ages is minimal. Interaction with children, young people, and middle-aged people will be limited and depend largely on visitors. Because of the high average age, the death rate will be higher than elsewhere.

Often new residents of such colonies rejoice at first that all the neighbors speak the same chronological language and take an interest in the same things. But this rejoicing can be brief as the realization comes that one is, henceforth and forevermore, hemmed in by contemporaries. Possibly the only way to "have our cake and eat it, too" is to find such a retirement complex with its peculiar advantages that is situated on the edge of a standard community and within easy reach of stores, churches, and places of recreation.

The disadvantage of spending so much time with persons our age is our tendency to become ingrown. A few may find it possible to keep abreast of current events, but in a colony of our peers the temptation is to live in the past. We are less likely to be shaken out of our comfortable cocoon by new words, new ideas, new action, new fashions, and new approaches. For newness and freshness we need to associate with people younger than ourselves. On the other side, if we are withdrawn from younger people we shall miss the chance for contributing to them the stability and worth of our experience.

The extreme opposite of being hemmed in by contemporaries is to be trapped where there are scarcely any people our own age. This can happen if we settle in a new subdivision where young people and their children represent the large majority of the inhabitants. The pace of neighbors may well tire us simply by watching the activity. We could not possibly share their normal routines. We might have the satisfaction of having some of these younger people come to us for counsel, and we might find opportunities for being helpful to them, but this will not compensate for our loss by being cut off from people our own age.

The happiest place to spend our older years would be one where a wide range of ages are represented, along with a good mixture of races and occupations. This kind of living place makes possible a give-and-take which is essential for the best mental health, and good mental health will result in better physical health for us.

Making the Best of It

As we think carefully over the social changes that lie ahead, some ways of adjusting wisely will occur to us.

We can resolutely decide to expand our circle of *acquaintances as far as feasible* considering the alteration of our circumstances. Each of us must make his own social life to a large extent. Unless we push out and enlarge our social contacts and experiences our existence will become dreary.

To push out the circle requires energy and thought and initiative. Where to begin?

Family comes first despite any arguments or rifts that may have occurred. A circle that omits family (if any are living) has a great gap in which nothing else can be placed. The family is the larger nucleus of which the individual is the center. Our circle should not be limited to the immediate family but should extend, in biblical terms, to the "third and fourth generations." When the family has dwindled some resemblance of family is retained by continuing to display pictures of those who have died. The memory of former friendship and shoulder-to-shoulder encounters with the world serves as some substitute for the loss.

Beyond the family center extends what we might term the "inner circle." Here we put our confidants and close friends. And how fortunate we are if we have a few of these to whom we may go when the world seems to press in unusually hard, when we have misgivings concerning ourselves or the future of mankind, when we need to check our convictions against those of others whose judgment and integrity we have come to respect! This part of our circle should never be allowed to shrink. And if we are to enjoy this type of relationship we must be the kind of people that others will want to have in their own "inner circle." We also need to cultivate new friends who may, in time, replace those we lose by death or through moving away.

Our circle will include less intimate friends, acquaintances whom we enjoy seeing regularly, old associates in our profession, our doctors, the merchants and clerks with whom we deal, the members of our church or synagogue or other place of worship, community officials, neighbors, and even passersby whom we greet occasionally.

Some of those in our circle we know because we live with them. Some we know from intimate conversations and shared experiences. Some we know from professional or mercantile dealings. Some we know from a more casual relationship.

We need to work at pushing out our circle as far as is feasible, recognizing that too large a circle is hard to maintain, and too small a circle impoverishes the soul. We must work hard to keep our associations fresh and friendly.

Related to the formation of our personal circle comes a second way of making the best of our condition — *listening*.

The opposite of listening we know all too well — incessant talking! But the world is crying out for listeners. This cry for a listener we often interpret as "noise." The fire siren with its accompanying rush of engines and police cars and ambulances — listen to the disaster that has struck some home or person or business! And the blare of cars horns — listen to one who is in a hurry and demands the right of way for one reason or another. The wind, the rain, the thunder — listen to nature taking care of the world and shaping and adjusting it. The television, the radio — listen to what has happened to mankind and to what mankind is doing in return. So many noises assail our older ears that we grow impatient and wish for quiet. And yet, listening to these noises with understanding helps us make the best of our contracted social world because we shall be mentally and emotionally in the thick of the action. Who would want to be a recluse in a sound-proofed room? Curiosity would rebel against such a sheltered existence, and curiosity is one of the health-giving attributes of our minds. Who can see a person with a bandaged arm or head or walking with a crutch without wanting to know, "Whatever happened to him?" By all means we must maintain this interest in what is happening to our brothers and sisters in the world if we don't want our aging to become a barrier to social contact.

But there is a more delicate listening that requires greater attention and thought. Noise is the indicator of the need for a listener. But under the noise is the real, and often heartbreaking, cry for someone to take the time to really listen to the hurts and frustrations of a person who feels bottled up without an outlet for his woes. If we are willing to listen, we may bring hope into another life and find an additional sense of usefulness and fulfillment for ourselves.

The art of listening does not come easily. How many times have married people heard wives or husbands declare, "You haven't heard a word I have said"? Of course we are polite enough to be quiet during the conversation of our spouse, but sometimes we get so involved with our own thoughts and concerns that we do not listen. As we grow older we may decide that we do have time to listen if we will. The penalty for not listening is a sort of solitary confinement since we will not know what others are thinking or feeling.

Patient listening could even become one of our best contributions to the social scene. The field for listeners is wide open, and all of us can improve in our ability to hear what is really being said. In recent efforts to improve listening and communication a simple plan has been used in small groups. All but one in the group wait silently while a speaker makes a statement. Then each of the members of the group, in turn, puts in his own words what he thinks the speaker was trying to convey. He starts out by saying, "I heard you say — and then expresses what came to him as he listened. Usually, no two people have perceived the same message. Rarely, does even one person come forth with a reasonable understanding of what was intended. The conclusion is that no one has the right to say that he has really heard a speaker until he can come up with a statement that the speaker will recognize as what he had in mind. True listening reaches beyond the actual words and gestures for the truth that a friend or acquaintance or stranger is trying to tell us.

The obvious first step in becoming a better listener is to discipline ourselves to be quiet while another is speaking. From there we must develop the ability to sense the overtones and "hear" even that which is not put into words. The better we come to know a person, the easier and more efficient will be our listening. Always we should remember that talking comes naturally, but listening skill must be acquired.

To round off our acceptance of the social changes of getting older, we might consider that pushing out among others calls for choosing our circle people wisely, and that we must *use care not to crowd ourselves or others*.

When we think about our social life, we need to decide where a place might be that will offer us the opportunities for the kind of contacts that are congenial to us. The choice of a "permanent home" will determine to a large extent the kind of people and the kind of opportunities available for our hoped-for social outreach. One pastor who had changed churches several times during his career retired and bought a small house which he named, "Dunmovin." To a degree this will be our experience insofar as we can control our life. We shall be done with moving. And when we move to the selected spot we must accept the fact that those we see around us are the ones who will make up our world to a great extent.

Of course, even in a new neighborhood we have the privilege of some choice. Our location will thrust some people upon us for good or ill, but even so, many of these will remain at a greater distance than those we choose to invite into the circles we have mentioned. And we will likely find that getting older has made possible new standards by which to select the ones upon whom we hope to bestow some of our time and energy. No longer need we draw the line so closely around those who are of our general religious persuasion, those who have comparable educational advantages, those who are in our general financial bracket, those of our race, and so on. Now our time is growing shorter and we may be more inclined to look at people for what they are, apart from outward accomplishments or adornments. We may be able to admire personal gold no matter what its setting. The older years offer so much of real and rich companionship because of this new outlook on the people who live in this same world with us.

We have been speaking of the quality of the people with whom we hope to interact in one way or another. Now we need to think of quantity — numbers. Medieval theologians sometimes speculated on how many angels could stand on the head of a pin! Given the size of the surface, how many ethereal beings could occupy it? To some extent we have this problem. The surface of our possible social life is determined by our health, our ability and desire to entertain, the time available to us, what we have to offer to others, and our ability to finance a program that we lay out for ourselves. We must be careful not to crowd our social surface with so many "angels" that our obligations become a burden instead of the joy that they should be to us.

Likewise, as we avoid crowding our own surface, we must be careful not to crowd the surface of others. If a doctor gains a good reputation for his skill and personality his office may become so crowded with patients that he cannot give each one the best care. And we might find some people in our small world that so appeal to us that we desire greatly to include them among our best friends. But if they are already loaded with family members and friends, it is better to keep our relationships with them casual and at their option.

Even the ones whom we do finally include in our social circle should not be so overwhelmed by our insistent attention that they have little time for their own chosen affairs. Nothing ruins a friendship or a family tie quicker than monopolizing. In effect we sometimes say to a person, "Now see here, I have chosen you as a friend. Remember that I come first!" This may work between two young people who decide to "go steady" but it does not work with older people who have other outlets and obligations, and whose emotional outlay and time must be widely distributed. This illustrates another reason why we should make our circle as large as our limitations permit. There is nothing so destructive as to think of our circle as a spider web in which we seek to entrap those whom we want near us.

MONEY

At all ages, the financial considerations of life must be admitted as legitimate and essential. Therefore, any complete investigation of getting older must include a close look at the amounts of money and credit available. Although we might like to shy away from monetary concerns as materialistic and gross, we cannot escape the hard fact that income represents the wherewithal of existence and the very lifeline of the older person. Indeed, the older person must take a closer look at his resources than the younger because it tends to be less flexible.

In younger years crises and shortages occurred but there was always the possibility of an increase in salary, a bank loan, or extra work on a temporary basis. In later years a man or woman rarely dares to borrow money that will place an even greater strain on his resources, he or she has no steady job (as a rule) that might bring in more, and the chances for going out into the labor market are slender and not too remunerative. To use a biblical illustration, Samson lost his strength when his hair was shaved off, but he thought his physical resources were as unlimited as before and said, "I will go out as at other times, and shake myself free" (Judges 16:20). But he soon found that the days of extra strength were over and he was made a slave. So with our change of circumstance.

We must look carefully at our financial picture since we cannot scurry around and improve it as easily as we once did, and we must avoid enslavement to money worries.

The Good

There are, as we shall see, some favorable aspects to the financial reappraisal as we get older. For one thing we will find that our *obligations and wants are fewer*.

That word "obligation" is a harsh one, but it expresses the reality of our earlier situation. A husband or wife has obligations to the spouse. Parents have obligations to their children (a recent estimate of the cost of a child from birth through college places the figure, conservatively, at $35,000 to $50,000). There are obligations to church, charity, community projects, and tax structures. Further obligations grow out of maintaining a home, owning a car or two, assuming memberships and subscriptions, and the like. No matter how rich or poor the older person has been, he has the obligations that put a strain on his income.

As we get older many of these obligations diminish. Children become self-sufficient. Insurance policies (if any) have matured, or have earned enough dividends to make the premiums smaller. A smaller house or an apartment and a more modest pattern of living eliminates some expenses and reduces others. One car or no car at all can provide substantial savings. Taxes decrease proportionately with a lower income. If we had a mortgage or two these have been paid off or can be refinanced with much smaller payments.

Along with fewer obligations come fewer and less expensive wants as we grow older. We lose the inner pressure to "keep up with the Joneses" or any other family. Indeed the Joneses and Browns have quit trying to keep up with us as they have grown older! Clothing seems to wear longer because we are not engaged in so many activities. Luxuries — things we would "just die" if we could not have — lose their earlier appeal.

All in all, the postman brings us fewer bills that demand large and prompt payment.

Now we can settle down to a pattern of living on available income that will fluctuate with a minimum of change. *Social Security* is the anchor of our financial program. Anyone who has been an employee or who has been self-employed is likely to be entitled to an amount that will be close to $200 monthly — a bit less for some who have been retired for a while, and considerably more for others whose retirement is recent. Increases of this amount may be expected frequently as Congress reviews the cost of living. A widow will do quite well, also, even though she may not have been employed. Social Security combined with full

Medicare benefits is a sound and assuring base of the older person's financial needs°

Another financial asset for many older persons is some kind of *pension* from his or her lifework. The possibility of a pension is much greater now than in former years. The activity of labor unions, legal pressures from government, and insurance plans for the self-employed are raising the percentage of occupations including pensions as a fringe benefit.

With care, as will be discussed fully later in this chapter, the monthly checks from Social Security and pension funds can provide a sound financial base and relieve one's mind from undue anxiety about money matters.

A third source of retirement income, which used to be only for the favored few, is found in *investments*. Even the poorest of us may have managed some savings through the years in the form of building and loan savings, bank deposits, government bonds, stock certificates given by an employer or bought. Maturing insurance policies may have provided us with annuities or the money to make some small investments. At retirement these investments may be augmented if we own a house and sell it to buy a smaller house or go into an apartment. The surplus from the sale may be available to be put out at interest.

Frequently, investment interest can be augmented by those who own stocks or bonds by

---

°This paragraph refers to provisions in the United States. Other countries have arrangements that approximate Social Security and Medicare so that the conclusions given above apply roughly to the circumstance of readers wherever they live.

selling wisely and putting the capital gains (the amount that represents an increase over the original cost of the securities) and the original principal into other stocks or bonds. Most of us need expert advice on this sort of transaction.

Small amounts placed regularly in a savings account grow surprisingly fast if the interest can be left to multiply. If a capital gains sum offered by a mutual or other fund can be used to purchase more shares, income is increased significantly. If Christmas or other holiday and birthday gifts, anniversary remembrances, and the like come in the form of cash, these small amounts make a useful addition to a savings account.

Sometimes older people find it congenial and helpful to take *part-time work*. As has been noted, the market for those of us of mature years is not so brisk as that for younger people, but there are opportunities for which we may be especially adapted. We might well look at some of the possibilities.

If the older person has been employed, the former employer might have an opening. The employer knows your capabilities and might hire you to fill in during the vacation or illness of a full-time worker.

Neighborhood shops and markets may welcome an older person whose income needs are not great and who would be willing to work on an irregular basis.

Many communities prefer older people as crossing guards at school intersections and scale the pay to assure the worker an opportunity to make at least the amount allowed by Social

Security without loss of benefits.

If the older person would like to combine his daily walking discipline with house-to-house surveys or solicitations of a commercial nature some income is possible.

And if the financial or psychological need for employment is acute, the older person may find in the phone book the names of agencies specializing in finding work for the "past 60" people in the area.

There are some things to be said in favor of a "job" of some sort. First of all, the job is a bonus in a sense, if it is not the prime source of income and the older person knows that he can live in reasonable comfort without it.

Also there is now time to enjoy the work undertaken. Instead of thinking of the job as a stepping-stone to something, we may relish what we are doing and appreciate those with whom we work. There is less pressure since the employer or agency took into account our limitations when we were hired.

Some of this earlier pressure was due to competition. Always in younger years we knew that if we did not deliver well, someone was breathing down our necks who would like to take our place. This is not as true now. On a part-time job the salary or wage is likely too small to excite much competition.

Another "good" aspect to our financial situation is that *expert advice is available* to us when we need additional funds or seek to ascertain the wisest way of utilizing any surplus we may have. Because we are classed among the older people

Money

in society, advice is given gladly, often without fee.

The bank where we cash our checks and transact our other banking business is glad to advise on ordinary problems and can direct us to other agencies for specialized advice. We may feel free to approach any of the officials who sit at desks behind the railings — usually near the front door. We shall receive courtesy and concern from these people since it is to their advantage to keep their older customers satisfied.

If we have made a will (a "must" for everyone growing older), the lawyer who helped with this instrument will be glad to provide additional counsel. He will refer us to someone else if our problem is not in his field of knowledge. A busy lawyer may make a small charge for his services.

The local Social Security office is exceptionally helpful and friendly. Frequently special benefits are available of which we are not aware. A frank statement of our circumstances can do no harm and may do us some good.

If our problem is a matter of investment, a stockbroker or investment counselor in the community may well find it to his advantage to advise us concerning the most profitable way to dispose of any surplus funds. Or he may find that a present investment could be changed to increase the amount of interest.

Should the matter of a major purchase — of an appliance for instance — come up, consumer advice is available in many communities (call the county courthouse and inquire). Consumer magazines and annual guides are sold at newsstands and in supermarkets. Our favorite department store can be helpful in explaining the advantages of various brands, sizes, and models of merchandise. And we ought not to forget the Better Business Bureau as a source of advice.

The gist of all this is that no older person need bungle through any kind of financial problem and lose money through ignorance. Good advice is available and will be given gladly. We might compare notes with our friends regarding the various avenues open on certain problems if there is no need to keep the matter confidential. Others may know of sources of information that we have overlooked. They may help us avoid unnecessary expenditure and worry.

We should guard against that luxurious attitude of going our own way "asking nobody anything"! Only if our funds are unlimited can we afford that sort of independence, and even then such an attitude is probably not wise.

The Not So Good

Among the not-so-good features of our changed financial condition is the undeniable necessity for *reducing the level of living*. For some the difference may be drastic, for others barely noticeable, and for the majority a decent sort of comedown.

Rarely will the same housing be maintained, and if it is the utilization is likely to be curtailed. A family home of three or four bedrooms with bath facilities to match may be exchanged for a smaller house or an apartment. The less fortunate of us may have to do with one or two rooms. No

Money

matter how well we utilize the new space, at times the walls will seem to push in on us. And the difficulty of entertaining family members or house guests for overnight, or just for meals, will present some problems.

In the old situation, too, we may have enjoyed laundry pickup, milk and grocery delivery, personalized car-servicing, and the like. Now we may find that these were aspects of gracious living that can be dispensed with, and that by taking care of such details ourselves we can save many dollars. All "free" deliveries must be paid for after all, by charging higher prices for the services and commodities.

We may have had a habit of sending our garments to the dry cleaner after wearing them only a few times. Now by brushing and hanging carefully we can space the cleanings at greater intervals — and we may use spot cleaners without professional help. The same holds true for drapes and upholstery.

Another change will be in the number of memberships we hold and pay for. Since we are no longer obligated for business or professional reasons to be part of organizations or clubs, we shall be able to disappear from these circles. And the former choice of good seats at concerts or plays may have to give way to less expensive locations — the balcony, perhaps, if the steps are no great barrier.

The satisfaction and prestige of giving to community projects on the level of sponsor which included having our name printed in a program may need to give way to smaller gifts, shared on an anonymous basis.

If we have taken regular vacations, we must be ready to change our routine. Popular places written up in the travel pages of the paper, charging height-of-the-season rates, will not be for us. Less well-known and talked-about spots on an off-season rate can bring us just as much physical and mental renewal.

As we gear down to a reduced level of living we may find that we slip one or two notches on the social ladder. A few rich may be able to maintain their style of life, but most of them will slide into the upper-middle class. The former upper-middle may find themselves in the lower-middle group; the lower-middle may become genteel poor; the genteel poor too often, without regular salary or wages, will sink to subsistence level. Remember, though, that this change of living applies only to our financial circumstances and does not affect our worth as persons.

What it all amounts to is that a manner of living to which we have become accustomed must give way to a manner of living to which we are forced to become accustomed. This lowering of the outward level of living ought not to tax our pride too severely. As a matter of fact, this not-so-good aspect will bring some blessings with it. Tensions and pretence will be lessened. Salesmen and self-seekers will find us less lucrative as prospects. Even burglars may treat us with some contempt! And many of us will be settling back comfortably into a groove that we once occupied when we were on the way up years ago.

Forced to lower our level of living, we shall find

that *we must forego some familiar luxuries*. As younger people we may have demanded only the best. In an ad a man is shown selecting a luxury item in an exclusive shop. He is asked, "Do you know what that costs?" His answer: "What it costs? No, and I don't care. It's the best and that's what I want." If this has been our deliberate or subconscious approach to life, we must now be content with second-best, or even third-best. If we cannot bring ourselves to this change, we can hope to have the best but obtain it rarely and do without in the meantime.

In the food line this will be true. If we like meat daily, we won't be able to have filet mignon or tenderloin all the time. Ground meat and meat substitutes will be on our table more often. We'll find that we must hold back the appetite for seasonable things until they have been on the market long enough to go down to a more reasonable price. Instead of tossing out leftovers, we may find an additional meal in them.

As for our clothing, the same principle of avoiding the costly will be in order. Tailor-made suits and private dressmaker frocks (unless we have physical reasons that require these), garments with the label of a renowned designer, guaranteed one-of-a-kind items, apparel from exclusive little shops will be found impossible luxuries for us — and totally unnecessary. Our shopping will be for durability as well as for style. And, as for style, we will be cautious about adopting a new fashion when it first appears since we have learned by experience that we might be out-of-date in a few months and have our money tied up in clothing that we would feel embarrassed to wear. A smaller supply of clothing will be needed than when we were more active, and we shall find that we can endure wearing something that others have seen us in before!

Household furnishings and appointments will come under the same hard scrutiny. If we have moved from a larger to a smaller place we will have kept, of course, our best pieces. Replacements will be rare and on the utilitarian side. The acquisition of expensive objects of art must be left to richer folk, and we can satisfy our need for these by visiting art galleries and museums. Home or apartment alterations and redecorations must be controlled by the budget under which we plan our affairs, and must not be the result of whims.

If we think this departure from luxuries is hard to bear, it may help to remember that standards of luxury change with the years. For instance, the automatic clothes washers and dryers, refrigerators, and electric ranges many of us take for granted were considered luxuries by our parents. The same holds true of a television set, a modern radio, imported foods, and the new fabrics that require no ironing, and so on. Many possessions which we consider necessities were the mark of affluence only a generation ago. In reality we are on a high level of daily living compared to fifty years ago and compared to millions of people in underdeveloped countries of the world today. We have simply come to the point where we must let our children and their children worry about the "last word" in this or that, and about possessions which are status symbols.

This leads us into the not-so-good necessity for *"making do"* at times. If we are to maintain a healthy financial picture we cannot toss out all that we tire of or that becomes a bit worn. The philosophy expressed in the joke about a man who traded his car in for a new one because the ashtray was full is something we must avoid!

And while we are on the subject of cars, we might consider that a car is one possession that we can make-do with for many years. As we get older we drive fewer miles, shorter distances, and at a more moderate speed than in our more active days. Some insurance companies automatically reduce the insurance premium for drivers of sixty-five and over. If a car is serviced regularly, and if worn parts are replaced as needed, it will give many years of the kind of service we require. It is well to find a reliable mechanic or garage owner who does not sell cars and trust his judgment on the safety of our vehicles. Like our family doctor who comes to know our physical makeup, the same mechanic working on our car time after time gets to know its weaknesses and its merits.

In the house, cleaning and reupholstering will do nicely instead of discarding well-built chairs and sofas. Hardware stores sell simple kits for refinishing wood which can be used by anyone with the will to learn and some ability to work with the hands.

We can make-do with wearing apparel by realizing that it will give prolonged use if minor mends are made in time. Many community laundry and dry cleaning establishments maintain a tailor and/or seamstress and will do these bits of repair for their customers at a reasonable cost. Alterations and dyeing may rejuvenate a coat or dress when make-do is a necessity.

With limited money to spend on new things, a strict policy of make-do will bring us back to the ingeniousness of our pioneer or immigrant ancestors. A fringe benefit will be the feeling of thriftiness in a day of waste, when pollution by discarded items is becoming an appalling problem.

A final not-so-good aspect of our financial situation is that *emergencies are difficult to anticipate* and estimate. Of course there were many emergencies when we were younger, but often we had a general idea of what to expect. As we get older and live by couples, or singly, we look into a mysterious future not marked by the uniform experience of others our age.

At this point in life, emergencies may arise regarding our health. Aging brings with it a vulnerability to crises of our physical bodies. Just as a person who lives in an old house knows that the chances of suffering plumbing, heating, lighting, roofing, and gutter breakdowns are greater than for a man who has moved into a newly built home, so we need to recognize the possibility of experiencing more difficulties in our aging bodies. This does not mean that we must live in dread of what is to happen tomorrow, but that we must be realistic enough to know that emergencies may arise and may require expenditures.

In addition to health emergencies, there will be emergencies that affect our dwelling. A sudden decision by city or town council may increase our taxes sharply before we have time to readjust our budget. If we rent, the rent may be raised. A community building program may put us to the expense of moving. We may find it desirable to move because of changes in our neighborhood that add difficulty for people of our age to live in comparative peace and comfort.

Another class of emergencies has to do with illness or need in our family. We may be called upon to make an expensive trip to help out during a crisis. And this family problem may mean that we shall want to make a temporary loan to a loved one even out of our limited resources.

It is difficult to chart the various fields where emergencies might arise and, thus, to prepare for them all. Of one thing we may be sure, it is a rare older person who lives out his later years calmly and serenely with no breaks in the even progress of his life. And wouldn't it be a withdrawal from life, after all, to expect that kind of placid existence? A French author many years ago said that the worst thing about being laid to rest in a cemetery is that you no longer read the newspaper! Even though we are older we are not yet in the cemetery and we do read accounts daily reporting on minor or major disasters of one kind or another.

This possibility of emergencies calls for two unwelcome preparations. In the first place, we must not be tempted to commit our resources too heavily. In younger years we could purchase many items on credit. In addition we might have taken on a twenty- or thirty-year mortgage to buy a home, a three-year note to purchase a car, a five-year obligation for major home appliances, and spread college tuition over a ten-year period. All of this spending or investing was based on a regular and growing income. Now this pattern of life should be avoided in order that emergencies not find us with every dollar of income spoken for. If our possessions are unencumbered, some may be pledged as collateral or sold to provide quickly available cash.

The second preparation is to accumulate what accountants call a "sinking fund." For a businessman, such a fund is set aside from income to take care of replacements of equipment or property, and to provide for major repairs. If a man knows that a typewriter or other tool will wear out within five years, then an amount equal to one-fifth of the cost of a replacement must be added to the sinking fund each year. With us, depreciation cannot be so carefully calculated but we will be wise to lay aside as much as possible toward such emergencies as may arise.

Making the Best of It

By now, having reappraised our financial standing, we may feel a bit blue and hemmed in. There is some cheer about the whole thing, however, as we found when we listed the good points. And if we are determined to make the best of it our future can be not only bearable but enjoyable.

First, it will help to *know exactly where we stand*. Charles Dickens' novel, *Great Expectations*, emphasizes the value of taking stock. The young man, Pip, and his friend Herbert got themselves in debt. They had bills stuffed in pockets and drawers and scattered about their rooms, but they could only guess at how much they owed and to whom. Finally, Pip suggested that they look their affairs in the face. Both of the young men brought out a large sheet of paper and a pen and listed systematically the amount of each bill and the name of the creditor. Then the amount of the debt was totaled. The two improvident friends found that this frank acceptance of the real facts of their condition brought a calmness and peace even though they still owed the money.

We should stress this kind of procedure to ourselves. Setting down the income we can depend on each month will enable us to balance that income by the amount we can spend for food, our home, clothing, recreation, and so on. Facing reality openly will keep us from unhappy surprises in the days ahead. In addition to this kind of budgeting a daily listing of what we spend will give us a guide. After a month we can see the trend of our fixed needs. A listing for a year will give us a good pattern that will show both standard and occasional expenses. If we have any debts we should keep a notebook of some sort and show payments made.

A further recording of our finances should show our net worth: investments (if any), savings, value of any property owned, and the cash value of any insurance policies. This record will show us exactly what we can bring into play against emergencies, and may cool our desires for a "fling" or a "splurge" until we are well able to handle the unusual spending.

This determined assessment of what we have, what we will receive, and what we must expect to pay out will bring a solid feeling of integrity. We shall not be living in a dream world and we shall not be likely to become the victims of our whims and desires for unneeded things. Also, we shall be fortified against ads, prospectuses, and cheerfully insistent salespersons. We shall be completely aware of what we can and may do and what we cannot and must not do if we hope to live without a constant, gnawing anxiety.

There may be objections that this precise sort of living will take all our fun away and make Scrooges of us! Not at all. *Life will be wholesomely simple* as compared to the complicated financial manipulations of our younger years. This change will contribute to our good both physically and psychologically.

Anxiety accompanies financial carelessness. Even though we may have, sometimes, a secret wish to "blow the works" just once more, we shall have to admit that peace of mind which comes from living within income is a greater blessing than any ill-advised splurge in expenditure. To be able to know, day after day, that we have been faithful to ourselves and to all who might be burdened by us by courageously sticking to a program with our money is a tremendous aid toward possession of calmness and cheerfulness.

Instead of straining to make ends meet we shall see that, at last in our life, the ends *do* meet, and this without any superhuman effort on our part. The absence of a guilt feeling because of some folly in squandering a part of income that should have gone for true well-being will make for a healthful mental attitude. Despite all of our care, unavoidable events will come to cause us concern and worry. Why should we add worrisome things that can be avoided?

The unclouded mental outlook made possible by an uncomplicated financial routine will result in real physical dividends. A good night's sleep could be the reward of ending each day without a recorded deficit that we see no way of covering.

All bodily functions are benefited by the serenity of that part of thought affected by money matters. Physicians tell us that appetite, digestion, the nervous system, and blood pressure are all improved or impaired by one's mental attitude. We shall be helping ourselves in many ways by being reasonable in the handling of our funds.

In fact the body is better off when we do not indulge in many of what we mistakenly call the "good things" of life. Instead of rich, fancy foods we will choose to eat basic things in moderate quantities.

By making our expensive excursions few the body will be more likely to get sufficient rest and life will be longer and more worth having. And in these days of air pollution, the fewer gallons of gas we buy will not only save us fuel money but will help us avoid the fumes of thousands of exhaust pipes and result in better health for our respiratory organs.

By limiting our financial obligations to proper proportions, we shall find that physical demands upon us will be much lighter. We will not be called upon to exert ourselves in so many directions. We shall learn to put our strength against fewer and more worthy projects and have a happy feeling of completion.

As a last thought on how to make the best of our more or less limited financial situation, we might well look at the *good that can come by disposing of material things*. To use a term familiar to medical men, we might call this sort of disposal a "catharsis," a purifying or purging of the emotions.

For most of us the experience of moving has become familiar. And many of us must have been shocked at least once in our lives by the sheer bulk and weight of our household possessions! Was it possible that so many tons of stuff were necessary for the comfortable living of a few — now, perhaps, only two — people? How in the world did we manage to acquire so much?

But if a last move must be made as we get older, it is not likely that we can take our vast accumulation with us. What is to be done? The answer is simple. Dispose of all except what can be used effectively in good conscience and with joy.

First of all, plan to give away some things. Giving, of itself, has a wonderfully beneficial effect on the emotions. Each chair, table, lamp, bookcase, rug, file of magazines, toy, book, chest has a memory. To throw these things out or burn them would bring a great sadness. But we can give them away with the thought that the money and love we spent upon them will not be completely wasted if others receive some pleasure from the articles. Family, friends, charitable organizations, newlyweds, and libraries are possible recipients of our excess goods.

Some things may be sold. If there are good (especially antique or rare) pieces we may well find buyers and use the money to fortify our new financial situation. And we can rest assured that people who pay good money for items intend to use them with respect.

After giving away and selling what we can, we may well find a sizable accumulation of things that must be destroyed. This ought not to be heartbreaking. Whatever is not good enough to give or sell can have only emotional value and we are now committed to purifying our emotions. That is, we are determined to spend our emotions capital hereafter on fewer things that possess genuine value in our present style of life.

And so we come to our smaller place surrounded by the best and most useful of what our younger years, and our inheritance, have gathered together. We must have noticed many small homes and apartments, even single rooms in "homes" or retirement centers that seem elegant. Formerly, the pieces now concentrated in a small area were spread out in a large space and were lessened in attractiveness by cheaper and gaudier companions. Now the best has a good setting.

Having come to the consummation of disposing of things, there is a real peace in knowing that our bridge has been crossed and that now we can hope to continue as we are for some time. The sharp regrets and tugs at the heart that came of getting rid of memory-shrouded things will soon leave and we shall wonder why we ever permitted inanimate things to take a toll of our affections. With fewer things to care for and worry about our life will flow more smoothly.

RECREATION

One of the joyous things about getting older is the rediscovery of that vestige of the "girl" and "boy" outlook on life that has remained somewhat hidden in our more active years. However, there are times when we are not content to feel this return to simpler days but try to show others that we are "young at heart." This may express itself in men combing a lock of hair over the eyes (if there is any hair to comb!), and women copying some of the casual fashions of the girls in the neighborhood. We older people know that such outward signs will deceive no one, but they do speak to us for the moment of certain excitements that date back to our carefree days. A better proof of the existence of this perennial boy or girl in us is a new delight taken in games.

Games and other forms of recreation fill a large place in the life of the older person, and rightfully so. Now that the years of active struggle to "win" in life's serious contest have passed, there is a need to exercise this same competitive spirit against opponents in contests and games.

The Good

While the change by age in relation to recreational possibilities cannot be completely good, there are some favorable aspects that we may dwell upon. We start out by noting that our new relaxed time schedule means that *we no longer must cram our recreation into a weekend orgy kind of thing*, and that we are free to examine the "creation" part of the activity as opposed to its "wreck" potential.

One of the difficulties of our earlier years may well have been the accommodation between the need and urge for play and the lack of hours available. We had read that our natures required the release that comes by recreation — "all work and no play makes Jack a dull boy" — but we found ourselves bound to the wheel of what seemed to us the far more essential endeavors. How does a fully employed man or woman keep his or her place in the "rat race" and yet step off the treadmill that makes the economic wheels go around long enough to enjoy good times? Too often the answer has been to crowd a weekend with enough sports and games to last us for another week. This can be illustrated by the regular practice of one of my employers who owned a summer place at an ocean resort. He took his wife and children to the vacation home just as soon as school was over and left them there until September. He lived in the city during the week and on Friday evening traveled to the shore where he stayed until as late an hour as he dared on Sunday night. One Friday afternoon when he and I were the only ones left in the office, he asked me to send this telegram to his wife:

"Same time, same place,
 All set for a hell of a pace."

This "hell of a pace" graphically describes what many of us considered to be recreation in our former years. And this kind of pace was just as injurious to us as an orgy of overeating or drinking. It tragically betrayed the wholesome impulse that we had to play some games.

In our older years we can examine recreation leisurely and learn the splendid meaning of the word. The body and mind suffer injuries in the wear and tear and worry of the average routine of life. If unrepaired the body and mind will struggle valiantly to keep going respectably, but sooner or later there will be little left except a thin and solid "do or die" determination to keep going. The zest for living will be cooled and the vision of what life really is dulled. A re-creation of this body and mind is called for, and the means of such re-creation may be found in sports and games.

Even those whom we think of as obsessed with profit-making have found that their employees make more money for them, in the long run, if the effort and tension of the day's work is broken occasionally. This realization has resulted in shorter workdays, shorter workweeks, the coffee break, and firm-sponsored sports teams of various sorts. These "letup" benefits are just as valuable to a worker as his medical insurance, and they rank on a par with the paid vacation. Let us never forget that our minds and bodies continue to need these changes even when our work is self-controlled and not so arduous.

We now have the advantage, too, of the privilege of being *leisurely and selective in our recreational choices*. The man who went to the shore for summer weekends had to crowd into his feverish pace swimming, boating, fishing, partying, table games, and other pursuits. But we may, on the other hand, concentrate on one activity that appeals to us at the moment, knowing that we may enjoy other possibilities in our own good time. The contrast is similar to the pace of a chess game that may take hours to complete as compared to the skeet shooter who must be prepared to pull the trigger each time a target is thrown up into his sights. If the skeet shooter is not constantly on the alert and prepared he will miss a chance that cannot be retrieved. With us, there is always another time and we do not feel that we have missed something if we spread our recreation over a longer period or take in fewer projects.

To look at this leisurely approach from another angle, we might say that we no longer submit to a production line type of recreation. We may make of our recreation a masterpiece of sportsmanship because we are not rushed. We remember that automobiles come out of machines and through the assembly line at scheduled intervals as planned by industry, but immortal works of art take time and individual effort. We now cease to be professional "recreationists" and drop back to an amateur standing! The frenzy and the aim "to

Recreation

have fun if it kills me" leave us.

This leisurely approach permits a free selection of what we choose to do. We may follow our moods. And we drop some inhibitions. Men who had been told that it was "sissy" to knit or do needlepoint now engage in such pastimes if they wish. Women who were told that only men took up woodworking as a hobby now, unabashedly, run their lathes and power saws. Many businessmen and business and professional women, statesmen, and others have selected painting as their chosen recreation. Instead of accepting the seasonal and customary sports and games in their prescribed settings, we may now do what we prefer to do when we want to do it.

All of this may well result in *an exploration of the old things* that we know familiarly *and a tasting of some things that are completely new to us*. We say exploration because so many of the recreational pursuits that we followed in the past were largely engaged in because of social pressure. Now we may go into the reasons and values of what is offered.

This exploration may include the reading of books on the subject selected. A man or woman who has fished for pleasure may have ventured no further than to use the line and bait that older fishermen recommended. A bit of pleasant research will uncover the origin of fishing as a sport, suggest lures to try, and describe the merits of various kinds of lines and reels and poles. Charts may indicate how to determine where the fish are likely to be in many kinds of waters. The changes of weather and the seasons will suggest additional experimentation. The more the fisherman knows about his art, the greater amount of true creation it will afford him.

What has been said of fishing, by way of example, is true of all sports and games and hobbies. There are simple guides to be found, and more involved books available. In times when weather or health prevent active pursual of the favorite sport, this kind of exploration will be almost as good as the real thing.

Exploration may take the form of experimentation as well as research. Golf and bowling, for instance, are games that offer great rewards to those who practice. While getting exercise, the older person may go out on the golf links or to the bowling alleys at off hours and improve his style of playing. A chess player may collect from a newspaper chess problems to be worked out when there is no opportunity for a game with anyone.

Turning to sampling new things, the opportunities are endless. Often, combination game boards are sold in stores with the advertisement that fifty-seven different games may be played with the equipment included. And yet the purchaser is likely to play only two or three of the games because the others would be new to him. Many opportunities for new games and recreational activities depend only upon studying a few rules and directions.

And there are times when we may have said, "Oh, I could never learn to do that!" "That" may have been chess, landscape painting, wood carving, archery, or any of a hundred things. But how do we know that we cannot learn unless we try? And if we try and succeed fairly well we have added some accomplishment or skill that will break the monotony of a life pattern and that will make us acceptable to people who have made "that" a favorite pastime.

If we think that the possible sports and games are fairly limited in number, we need only look into an encyclopedia of such things. And if we have thought that the possibilities within a basic game or sport are few, we need only size up the bulk of any book — such as Hoyle's book on games — to convince us that the field of recreational patterns is an old and immense one. In addition to what is new to us, we might watch the ads at Christmastime to discover some newly contrived games and puzzles to add to our list. Two games that are widely known now — Monopoly and Scrabble — came on the market in this way not too many years ago.

There are good recreational possibilities that cannot be classed as either games or sports, but which provide the same release from the duties and obligations and necessities of life. First to come to mind is *television*. Of course television has suffered from its critics to the point that we may be a bit embarrassed (if not downright ashamed) to admit that we spend much time before what has been called the "boob tube." It might help us to remember that the critics spend more time in front of the boob tube than we do, and make a handsome living from it!

Television watching can become an art rather than the haphazard flipping of the dials that we engage in ordinarily. The newspapers publish the offerings on TV a week in advance, and from these schedules a home program can be drawn up that will offer a variety of educational features, drama, travel, documentaries, and pure nonsense. A person living alone finds that television watching helps overcome loneliness because of the companionship of the people on the screen. And two people, or more, can agree on programs to be viewed and enjoy what is seen and heard just as though they were at a concert or other public event.

A quieter pastime than television is found in *books*. And reading may call for some dusting off of habits. Frequently, people have been heard to say, "I don't know when I have read a book. You know how it is with so much to do — the TV, magazines, newspapers, people coming in. When is there time to read books?" But this attitude can result in the waste of a wonderful source of recreational joy. One of the absolutely good things about getting older is the opportunity for reading books that we have been wanting to read and never found the time for reading. Reading need not be done according to a plan, although systematic reading has its place, as we shall observe in the chapter on education. We can profit recreationally just by reading what we want to read when we are in the mood for reading it. We may find that we are reading five or six books on as many subjects at any given period. If we like our reading recreation to be more orderly, we can find courses of reading filed in our local libraries, in the guide to a set of encyclopedias, or in the bibliography pages of books on a subject that we would like to pursue.

If an older person has eye trouble, he may secure from local, state, and federal agencies the loan of "talking books." Talking books (other terms are used in some areas) are recordings of standard and new works of literature. An instument to play these records or tapes is provided without charge. Information on this service is available in public libraries and in the offices of local social agencies.

In addition to TV and reading, listening to *music* is highly recreational. Records available today are sensitive reproductions of the best performances of orchestras and soloists. The newer casettes and tapes require smaller playing instruments and allow for more portability. Listening to familiar music will bring back happy memories, and listening to less familiar music will prove a challenge in appreciation. An hour spent with music should never be thought of as wasted or unprofitable.

The Not So Good

There are some recreational limitations as we get older that are not so good as the interesting things we have been discussing. For one, we know that *the more strenuous sports of your younger years are pretty much out of bounds now*. Football, hockey, tennis, lacrosse, handball, boxing, skiing, and the like must come under close scrutiny. Only in exceptional cases will this variety of sports be recommended to us. Some exceptions may be made for an older person who has kept to one of these sports consistently through life — such as tennis. If tennis or some other form of extremely active recreational pursuit has been a regular part of an older person's schedule, then he or she might continue for a while within reason. But if a person has dropped the sport for a time, or has played spasmodically for a long period, it is wise to give it up completely.

While the reasons against participation in extremely active sports are fairly obvious, we may put them down as a warning.

The immediate physical drain of strenuous sports presents a real problem to older people. The heart and lungs are taxed; the muscles, particularly those of the legs and abdomen, are called upon for repeated flexings; and the joints must move rapidly for an extended period of time.

Added to the quick physical exertion is the danger of injury. Even ruling out contact sports such as football, there is always the chance for collision with other players or with walls, and the possibility of falls. The older body is inclined to a brittleness not known in younger years.

It is not rare to see a participant in a televised game of tennis panting and showing signs of complete exhaustion. If this is true of young athletes, what must it be of people of our age? As the years go on, the time required to "bounce back" becomes longer and there is the danger that there will never be a full return to former vitality.

Add to all this that the achievement possibility is small for us in active sports. In the "bifocal" age games with a rapidly flying ball or other object present a problem for the eyes. Slow reaction time to quick shifts in a game pattern is a handicap. Even though we may be competing against people of our own age, the total performance is not likely to increase our pride!

To sum it all up, if we are relinquishing our full day's work as being a bit beyond our strength and endurance and are moving into retirement, why shouldn't we extend that understanding of our limitations into other areas of life, especially where exhausting sports are concerned? The body is no more miraculous in sports than it is in the daily grind of industrial, commercial, academic, or professional labor.

Another not-so-good feature in this area is that *younger people are impatient with older partners*. When we are convinced that the true value of sports and games is the enjoyment and uplift of them, we can easily recognize that they become meaningless if we are under the strain of trying to keep up with and please a younger player. Sometimes this is nullified if the younger player is a beginner and knows that he is taxing our patience just as we tax his, or if he is very young — a grandchild, perhaps — who plays with awkwardness. By and large, however, the young partner will be at the achieving age.

Speed is one thing enjoyed by the young, as we well remember from our own zippier days. And speed is not one of the characteristics that improves with age. We may say to ourselves that we move as rapidly as ever. But if we take note when we are walking briskly (?) along the street that we are being passed by young people who seem not to be hurrying, we may get an idea of the imperceptible change in us. This slowness becomes awkward in sports or games where the young are included. When bowling, golfing — or even playing something as inactive as Scrabble — the older player will slow down the game so that it takes longer to play. The young find it difficult to wait their "turn."

Intolerance of the older person's perception time will cast a cloud over the game in which assorted ages are involved. We who are older need to give attention to our playing instead of responding automatically to challenges and emergencies as once we did. What the younger can take in at a glance may not be at all apparent to us. Eventually we make good decisions, but the young would have done as well without so much thought.

And the young partners may have a mistaken notion that they must make more allowances for us than we actually require. At Ping-Pong, for instance, what young person is going to "ace" the ball with a triumphant whack that will make it carom off the table so fast that we cannot see it, much less hit it? And this kind of slam-bang playing is sauce for younger players. If they must make allowances for some "mom" or "pop" they may feel virtuous, but it is no fun!

So we shall find as we grow older that younger players grow more and more wary of joining with us in games or sports. This hurts our self-esteem and limits our possibilities for pleasure since contemporaries are not always available. Often, too, if our contemporaries are ready and willing we may have the same impatience toward some of them as the young have toward us! Getting older takes its toll in different ways with all of us. But one thing we know: "those older people" are always more decrepit than "we" are!

Another difficulty, we must accept is the need to *pace ourselves in our recreation*. The man or woman who once took a day off for golf and played thirty-six holes finds that now nine are enough before a rest period must be taken, and frequently nine holes will prove to be all that can be enjoyed in a day. Now that we are older, we must heed the requirements of the body for sensible pacing.

A popular song includes the line, "I could have danced all night." Many have worked or played into the wee hours of the morning and have lived through it. But as older people we know that in all that we do we must not "dance all night" but take things in moderation.

There is a pacing of the amount of energy that we may safely expend at one time. When President Kennedy's administration promoted fitness programs a challenge was put forth by some officers that their men join them in a fifty-mile hike. For the younger men this was possible, but the older men had to do the fifty miles on a start-and-stop basis. It turned out to be more than a one-day affair.

There is a pacing of time, also. A certain portion of each day ought to be devoted to some physical recreation for all of us in reasonable health. The amount of time will vary depending on what our experience has taught us is best for our physical and mental well-being. Often it is wise to divide our daily exercise into two periods — possibly one in the forenoon and one in the afternoon.

Pacing can be helpful for the mind, too. Perhaps we are inclined to think that the mind never tires as does the body. But experience teaches us that pushing ourselves for a long period of concentration on chess, crossword puzzles, reading a scholarly book, or whatever, makes us tired and nervous. No doubt there is value in giving the mind a brief rest when the freshness of our interest dulls.

Another aspect to pacing is worth considering. Absorbing things that are good and enjoyable in smaller doses will bring greater and longer-lasting satisfaction than a speedy, greedy approach. This is as true of recreation as it is of eating, drinking, talking, and other desirable pursuits.

A last not-so-good thing about our recreational possibilities as we get older is that *the reward element is almost gone, since there is not so much need for change*.

In younger years when we worked hard all day, an evening of recreation with family or friends repaid us for the long hours of unremitting labor that we had put in. Anticipating the evening's activities made the day more bearable. We had something to look forward to.

Plans for some recreation over the weekend offered a splendid return for the five or more days given to our required "earn-a-living" or "keep-the-house" occupation. Just as we looked ahead to a pleasant evening, concentrating on the weekend activities to come relieved some of the tedium for our long workweek.

Beyond the evening and the weekend, as the year went on, we could anticipate the reward of a vacation — one week, two weeks, or a month, maybe — which would be ours to use as we pleased. This meant "getting away from it all" in a real way. Even the burdens of the home and the neighborhood could be left behind as we set off for the shore, the mountains, or a camping area. Always at the end of our work tunnel — daylong, weeklong, or yearlong — we could glimpse the light of a break in the routine.

But now that we are older and more nearly retired, what is there that we are doing for which we should receive the reward of recreation? One older man was asked by a young friend, "Aren't you taking a vacation this year?" The answer was, "Vacation from what?" There is no doubt that the reward factor and the anticipation of a needed and welcome change are no longer as valid as when we were slugging away at a demanding career. And when we do go through the old motions of planned recreation we may have a little bit of the feeling of a truant from school. A holiday from school was earned and thoroughly enjoyed, but to skip school and take an unearned day brought a sense of guilt.

We shall have to learn to live with this different aspect of our recreation and find new values. Perhaps we should find a new category. We have talked about recreation relieving us from our work during an evening, weekend, or our annual vacation. Why not think of our recreation now as the reward of a *lifetime* of effort? Even though the need for pleasure may not be so acute as formerly, nevertheless we can find joy in remembering that we are not actually dropouts or truants from the world's work. Our job is completed and our more leisurely days are appropriate in light of the contribution we have already made to mankind. Never should we give way to the feeling that we are parasites and have no right to enjoy life.

Making the Best of It

Even though we may not be able to do everything in the recreation line that we wish we could, there are enough possibilities to keep us from boredom. Wallflowers we need not be. A wholesome exercise for us would be to *list the things we can do successfully*.

The list might start off with the most active sports we can reasonably handle. As we have noted, for those who have kept up their tennis without a break through the years this sport is permissible. People in their eighties including a Scandinavian king — have enjoyed this game. They play with moderation and in a style suited to their years. With some, doubles is a less strenuous game than singles. Fencing is another possibility since it calls for more skill than strength. Bowling is appropriate for most of us, and has the advantage of providing physical exertion on an extended but not continuous basis. For women a ten-pound ball is good. For men twelve or fourteen pounds may be better than the standard sixteen. In consultation with our doctor, a jogging program may be set up. Golf, of course, is good for both men and women. However, golf offers only small physical returns if a riding cart is used. It is the walking that is of great value. For men who enjoy it, hunting is an active sport and not too demanding if done in moderate weather. Shuffleboard, and bicycle riding are enjoyed by older people. Each of us will have other activities to add to the list.

For the "in between" — those sports or games that are not really strenuous but are not at all sedentary — we might start off with Ping-Pong (table tennis). This can be played indoors no matter what the weather may be, or outdoors on a porch or patio. Badminton offers good competition without undue exertion. Croquet may seem old-fashioned but it has a fascination that never dulls, and it draws in the neighbors! Quoits or horseshoes, lawn bowling or archery on a small scale may be added to this intermediate list. Here again, each of us will have some other favorite to add.

Then for the quiet activities our list could be nearly endless. There are Monopoly, chess, checkers, Scrabble and other word games, Chinese checkers, dominoes, charades, puzzles, crosswords, card games, backgammon, Parcheesi, and so on and on. Recently, game manufacturers have been specializing in adult games. Games dealing with social problems and psychological interests are available. And the old game of crokinole is appearing again in department and sporting goods stores. Major sports such as football, basketball, and hockey can be played on electric boards.

Beyond these three lists are contrived sports such as treasure-hunts, nature or bird hikes, com-as-you-are parties, progressive dinners, and the like.

By making lists such as these for ourselves tailored to our own situation, the temptation to get into a rut is lessened. If, when friends come for the evening, we bring out the one and only game that we like to play there may be a dull time for someone. For ourselves and our guests there should be a great variety.

Another excellent way of making the best of our recreational limitations is to *pick one thing* from among all the others on our lists *and determine to master it* so well that we gain the respect of all ages.

The selection of this one thing should be judged first by the pleasure that it gives us. Selfishness is a virtue here. It would be sheer boredom to concentrate on something that does not appeal to our interests. The choice might fall on either a sport or game.

Another test for our selection would be our natural ability to do the thing. If a sport, we should consider if we have the necessary dexterity. If a game, we should be honest in assessing our aptitude for the requirements of that pastime.

A third test would be the availability of space or opportunity for frequent involvement in the form of recreation chosen. For instance, if we decide on becoming expert in bowling we would need to be near enough to alleys so that we could go often for practice. If the choice is Ping-Pong we will need willing opponents or a "play-back" table for solitary practice. Games usually call for opponents, although we can play ourselves sometimes. A game such as chess can be improved by working out problems found in books or newspapers.

Once the sport or game is decided upon, a start

toward proficiency should begin by a trip to the local library (if we are physically up to this kind of excursion) or to a bookstore to look for books that give the history of the pastime and instructions for its play. A history of the sport may be read and returned to the library, but a book that gives instructions should be purchased for frequent reference. If your skill improves, progressively advanced books will be needed to keep pace with your new ability. For instance, a book on, "How to Improve Your Golf," by one noted player will not include all of the techniques. The advice of other famous golfers should be considered as well.

After one is familiar with the theory of the game or sport, long and patient practice is necessary. Just as a musician cannot perform without practice so a sportsman or gamesman cannot play well without doing over and over the steps in the playing. After you have mastered the basic techniques of the game, you will enjoy personal experimentation on new ways to improve. Take chess as an example. Every master of the game has produced some opening, middle, and ending of games that had never been recorded before.

The satisfaction of being able to defeat younger people as well as contemporaries in one sport or game is chiefly that of being respected for the skill and to know that the years have not taken away the ability to improve and learn when the mind is determinedly set on the task. Even to those of us unable to walk, this prospect of being exceptionally good at something is open.

At this point we might look at hobbies. As contrasted to sports and games, hobbies represent solitary and individual pursuits for the most part, and lend themselves to all kinds of physical conditions. Hobbies fall into two general classes: collecting and creating. We should *recognize the creative aspect of hobbies* and not treat them as ways of killing time. Whenever we older people come to the point where life is such drudgery that we welcome anything that will kill time and erase the hours, we are in a sad plight, indeed. Hobbies do much more than put a day away. They make a day exciting and too short. They offer opportunities for new knowledge and give us a chance to make another contribution to the world. Hobbies can be truly recreative.

Familiar hobbies of the collecting variety include collecting stamps, coins, books, china, pottery, figurines, historical objects by periods, recipes, minerals and rocks, and hundreds of other things. To make collecting educational and something of skill, most collectors narrow their field so that it becomes more exacting. If, for instance, a man or woman collects stamps there is little challenge since every stamp qualifies. But if he or she collects stamps of one country only, or of one period in the history of that country or on certain topics the search for what is wanted becomes more exciting. The same is true of books. Collecting books on one subject, or by one author, or first editions only is adventuresome. A collection of historical objects may be confined, let us say, to New England between the years 1750 and 1800. A collection of figurines may be of elephants only. And so it goes. The narrower the field of collecting the more the fun, stimulation, and excitement.

The creating kind of hobbies will include wood carving, sculpturing, painting, doing needlework, making ceramic pieces, furniture building, or refinishing, interior decorating, flower arranging, glass-blowing, sewing and dressmaking, photography, creative writing, and scores of other things. As with the collecting variety, these hobbies are best when confined to a special field. Many people have the same general hobbies. To be different enough to get real satisfaction and have something "to show" we will need to be specialists in some way.

The knowledge that comes from pursuing these hobbies will be similar to that of a student doing a specific piece of research. We shall need to read on the subject and compare with others as we continue on through years of enjoyment. Indeed, we shall need to resist the demands of the hobby or it may take over our life! Stamp collecting is good, but who wants to be known only as a collector of stamps? Common sense must call a halt if the hobby becomes an obsession. It is intended as a recreation and not the occasion for another major lifework.

The contribution we shall be making to the world will consist of the new knowledge that we add to what is known on various subjects and which we pass on to others. The collections or created pieces that we leave behind us may be the proud and useful possession of individuals or museums. A great part of the richness of the collections of libraries and museums is composed of the gifts of people who have taken the time to seek out scattered things and bring them together in one place. The handicraft of people such as ourselves may be examples to coming generations.

EDUCATIONAL OPPORTUNITIES

As we begin to look at the educational challenge of our later years we need to be sure that we are free of the mistaken notion that education is either a commodity to be obtained or something that can be finished. For instance, I talked with a man and woman of meager circumstances concerning their son who was away at college. They said that they had sacrificed for years so that their boy might "get" an education. This is an example of seeing education as a commodity.

We slip into the habit of saying of others, "They 'have' an education." A little thought convinces us that this conception is wrong. Education is a process that is never completed. It is important that we hold on to this truth as we get older. We are tempted to think of ourselves as "being" educated people, and that, for better or worse, the whole thing is done and there is nothing more we can do about it. The fact is that older people can profit as much from learning as the youngest child in the neighborhood. Diplomas on the wall or academic degrees attained should not be allowed to mark the end of our education. We shall do well to look closely at the possibilities for continuing our education in these mature years.

The Good

One of the good things we find is that *job-related study is no longer necessary*. Many times in our younger years we were tempted by tantalizing subjects that we wanted to pursue, but we were on the "time-machine" and had just so many hours available for study. The major portion of these efforts had to go toward refreshers and advanced courses in our own line. Even the simplest job required some cramming to keep us from getting behind and in danger of failure. Now that the job is behind us, we can venture down some of the fascinating roads to knowledge that were shut to us before.

And some of us who were bound by our vocations in this way are in greater need of digging into a general approach to education than those who needed to spend only a minimum of study time on "keeping up." Doctors, engineers of many fields, accountants, administrators, lawyers, to name a few, are among those whose task demanded continual study because of new developments, and what they learned in this process did not add appreciably to their general education.

If our work called for a somewhat narrow approach to the riches of the educational field, or if our job left us too exhausted at the end of the

Educational Opportunities

day to engage in cultural enrichment, we may be free at last to broaden our interests.

Many fields of study are available to us through adult education programs. No matter what the level of our earlier achievements or when we had to give up formal training, we shall find places and courses to help us go on from where we left off. A *review of classes open to us* may start us off well in our investigation. Day classes in high schools are open to older students if they have the courage to walk the halls and sit in rooms with young people who might be their grandchildren. Newspapers and magazines report such instances occasionally. But, to be with our contemporaries, we may prefer high school night classes if we do not have a high school diploma. In most communities high school credit courses are available in one or more of the local schools.

If we are at the level of undergraduate work, attending college day classes will not be as embarrassing to us as high school because there will be a greater proportion of older students. Even though a class is on the freshman level, it often draws more mature people who missed that particular course while going to college, and others who may need the subject for a teaching certificate or as a base for graduate work. However, colleges also offer evening sessions. In fact, a few colleges offer nothing but evening work.

Graduate work for those of us who may have a college degree offers a real challenge. Master's and doctor's programs are often undertaken by older people.

It is likely, though, that most of us have little

interest in credit courses and prefer professional instruction in something which intrigues us as a leisure activity. For instance, a man or woman whose hobby is minerals or rocks might well register for a course in geology or mineralogy. Such courses may be found in the listings of the adult schools arranged by every up-and-coming community. Usually the high school buildings are utilized for these schools and the staff is on a high level of competence. The range of subjects is broad: sewing, typing, languages, history, government, great books, creative writing, social sciences, and the like.

In addition to local opportunities, many correspondence courses are available. Home study schools now must qualify for state or national approval, as a general rule, which keeps the training at a respectable level. If you aren't sure about the legitimacy of an advertised school, a letter to the state Department of Education will bring an appraisal. Correspondence schools make possible educational pursuits by older people who are housebound or who live too far from ordinary schools to attend them conveniently.

A rapidly developing means for continuing education is the television used as a means of instruction. A number of universities plan annual opportunities for people to study at home under the mail direction of staff professors. This often involves filling out a detailed registration form, paying a fee, auditing twelve weekly lectures (usually at an early morning hour), and preparing a paper or taking a test.

Another opportunity to secure help in our educational plans is found in private tutoring. Among our acquaintances we may find a retired teacher in a field that is of interest to us. Or we may apply to our local board of education for the names of tutors whom they can recommend. We can watch the ads in the community newspaper or insert an ad of our own. Tutoring is particularly suited to those who desire to study vocal or instrumental music, to those who wish to improve their golf, and to other interests that do not yield themselves so well to class instruction.

In our educational plans, *books can become exciting tools*. Books are accessible in various locations. First of all, our own home has books of various kinds that we have acquired through the years. Our collection of books may be proportionately larger than the other possessions that we have kept. This is true for several reasons. For one thing, there is something about a book that causes us to pause before we discard it. It is, as a paper and cloth, a material thing. But there seems to be something beyond the material about it. We find that we can give a book to someone or donate it to a library but we cannot throw it away in the trash as we can other things! Others of our books are fastened to us by memories — we used them in school long ago, or they were the Christmas or birthday presents from our family or friends. Our collection has been made larger by the purchase of books and they represent real investment.

Beyond the home bookshelf is the library or libraries in the community. Even small towns usually have some collection of books for public borrowing and use. Nearby metropolitan areas have larger libraries and will grant guest privileges to nonresidents, sometimes requiring a small fee. If there is a college or university close at hand, its library may be used for reading if not for withdrawal.

"Flea" markets and rummage sales provide excellent opportunities to buy helpful books at minimal cost.

Some stores maintain lending libraries featuring current titles which may be borrowed for a small fee.

Without any great effort, we may lay out a reading plan in any field that we decide to venture into as a new educational challenge.

Perhaps our first encounter in any new area of learning (other than physical skills) will be with reference books such as dictionaries, encyclopedias, atlases, and almanacs. These books will outline our subject briefly and provide us with titles of books that are considered authoritative.

Earlier we looked at the possibilities for engaging in class and course work. Now we may consider if we want to use books as supplements to schoolwork or as our only aid in the learning. If classwork does not appeal to us, or physical or financial reasons are against it, a good plan of reading will prove to be a fair substitute. If we need courage to do the studying by ourselves we might remember that Abraham Lincoln had only books in his learning efforts and his use of those books changed him from an untutored child of a frontiersman into a man of broad knowledge and understanding.

As we get older and have time for making books tools as well as a means of recreation we may well be amazed at what we have been missing. A re-reading of just one solid book that we read earlier in life just for "fun" will serve to demonstrate how much we missed of an instructive nature.

Another good thing about our new educational challenge is that we have *time for travel*. Not all of us, of course, can take advantage of this privilege because of physical or financial limitations. Some of us can "travel" only through reading, watching television, and the sharing of experiences of others. But for any of us who can travel there will be an advantage beyond other forms of training. Our schools have recognized this value of late years and recommend that a pupil be sent abroad for one year of his high school or college training. Some colleges have gone so far as to make a year of study abroad a required part of the curriculum. In a most pleasant way travel can aid in our educational efforts.

Travel need not be restricted to trips abroad, however. Our own country offers much because of the wide variety of cultures and natural marvels available.

Travel exposes us to situations where people live differently than we do. Their ethnic background produces approaches and outlooks on life that are novel to us. Travel is educational. We can visit places where notable events occurred and where famous people lived. When we read, or listen to a lecture, we can imagine what the situation must have been, but only when we stand on the spot can we fix in our minds the true circumstances. Too often our imagination distorts the historical events or biographical achievements. A good illustration is the picture that many religious people have of the Holy Land. When they visit Palestine and Jordan, and the surrounding country, they are amazed at how small the sites of the Bible stories are and how short the distances from place to place. One can read about the Grand Canyon in school books but cannot possibly take in the scope and magnificence and coloring without standing on the rim of that tremendous gash in the earth. Thus travel brings perspective.

Happily, travel in our day is not so expensive as it was only a generation ago. Round-trip air fare for one or two to Europe or other continents is not prohibitive to many older people. Travel in our own country by car or bus, as well as by air, is surprisingly cheap. By being thrifty through the year, or over a period of several years, many older people may yet realize their dreams of seeing one or more of the great cities of the world or of exploring the wonders of their own country.

As older people, we may do our traveling in the "off season" when the fares on ships and planes are at their lowest, and when the hotels cut their rates for tourists.

Many reputable agencies offer group travel plans that decrease the cost even further and relieve one from the trouble and worry of making all the arrangements personally. In groups the older person has a sense of being looked after, which is comforting and especially helpful in case of emergencies.

The Not So Good

Although we approach our educational challenge with some enthusiasm, we will find that *personal discipline is harder to maintain* than in earlier years. Educational plans of any kind require a certain amount of study time and application. We have found that the process of getting older relaxes the sense of urgency in life. Our new pattern of doing what we please when we please is not conducive to a disciplined approach to a serious study project.

This "easy does it" attitude will first appear when we consider a course of study. The catalog from the local Adult School will come and we will seize upon it with eagerness. Of course we are going to enroll! Now, let's see what we want to take. But in the catalog there is a set deadline for registration and before we know it (and perhaps to our relief!) it is too late for *this* semester. This can easily happen semester after semester, and year after year. The same procrastination will be true of independent plans for reading, for getting up early enough to audit a TV course, or for beginning a correspondence course. We find it hard to pin ourselves down to something that represents any kind of rigid schedule.

And if by great effort we do take the plunge and enroll as a student somewhere, or if we do chart a reading plan, we'll think up all kinds of excuses for making exceptions. We'll find something that just must be done around the house, an errand that is urgent, a visit that must be made at precisely the time when the study was to have taken place. At first we'll console ourselves that we can "make up" the missed session by doubling our efforts the next day. Soon classes or reading periods missed will be so numerous that we'll feel justified in quitting with the promise that "next time" things will be different.

In addition to our general letting down as we get older, the difficulty of discipline is increased by our having no authority over us. Earlier study was under the eyes of the community, backed up by compulsory education laws, parents, employers, and others. If we did not fulfill our obligations on time, there were penalties. Now we are the only supervisors of our actions and we are inclined to be quite lenient and permissive with ourselves!

Admittedly, we do work under some handicaps. The mind and body are not so fit and trim and receptive as in younger years. Our efforts to keep on the course must be greater.

Also, *the incentive to learn new things is not so great* as before.

Earlier the incentive of progress was always before us. We must finish grammar school to go with our friends into junior high, and we must finish junior high to get into high school, and complete high school to gain etnry into college. Always there was the need to keep up with the crowd because we had a definite goal ahead that depended upon today's accomplishment.

A greater incentive, perhaps, was to become independent. We wanted to be in a position to buy our own clothes, get a car, have an apartment or home of our own, marry, have a family, be able to contribute funds to worthy causes, and be known as self-supporting.

Later, there was the incentive of getting ahead in our profession. If more education was the answer, then we plunged into it without fail. The fear of staying in a mediocre job or of remaining well down the ladder of success was a tremendous driving force to keep us from indolence.

And there was the incentive of becoming a fuller person. If education was the secret to understanding ourselves, life, and the people with whom we lived and worked, then education we must pursue. If education meant enrichment that would tide us over the low places in life, then we would steel ourselves to the necessary sacrifice and labor of study.

Now we do not feel the strength of any of these incentives as once we did. Where, for instance, is our progress? We have completed our major life plan. What lies ahead of us does not depend on more education at our time of life. It would be difficult to think of any future doors that might open because of our improvement in one branch of learning or another.

And, certainly, we are no longer working toward independence. We are about as independent as we will ever be. If we are becoming more dependent it is not likely that more education will change our status.

No longer do we need improvement in our work or professional skills. Either we are retired or so close to it that advancement is over so far as we are concerned.

There remains, however, the last incentive — that of becoming a fuller person. No matter how old we are, our potential for personal growth is not frozen. Anyone may continue improving himself or herself right up to the last competent day of life. I watch a news program on TV that flashes, "More, More, More," on the screen when a station break or commercial interrupts. We might think of ourselves in this way. No matter what the interruptions of getting older, retiring, going through losses and illnesses, we can always be confident that there is "More, More, More" within us.

Sometimes psychologists startle us by calculating that we use only a small part of our total potential. For instance, they claim that we utilize only one tenth of the capacity of the brain! And doctors tell us that we have a surplus of physical organs beyond what is absolutely necessary to life (two lungs, two kidneys, etc.) and that we utilize only a small proportion of our available strength. There is more of us than we have found. Our "inner person" also, has never risen to the peak of performance and possibilitites. If we are convinced that educational endeavors will help our inner self come more fully into its own, this will provide adequate incentive for study.

But just as we come to this stout conclusion, another not-so-good factor of getting older springs out at us: "Suppose we do gain *more knowledge and understanding, what will we ever do with it?*" I knew a woman who, at the age of seventy-nine, enrolled for the standard three-year course in a theological seminary and completed the work at the age of eighty-two. I asked myself, "What will she do with that training?" Certainly she could not stand the rigors of a parish ministry even if she could find a church that would take her on at

Educational Opportunities 121

that age. She was beyond the acceptable age range for teachers. Why, then, did she bother to study so long and so hard? What will she ever do with what she has learned? And so we ask ourselves of our much smaller plans for education: what will we ever do with the additional knowledge and skill?

We know that education cannot be stored up to bequeath to our children or friends. Education is a personal process and achievement. And we have ingrained in us a practical strain that always wants to know the good and the profit of whatever we strive for. Why spend so many dollars and so many hours of life advancing our education? What will come back to us as a fair return?

This practical side of us goes on to inquire what the added skills and abilities and understanding will "do." Suppose we learn all about the art of the sixteenth century. Suppose we learn how to recognize and name every tree and flower that we see. Suppose we master some musical instrument. Suppose we gain a general grasp of the philosophical teachings of the ages. What will these things "do"? Our own sense of personal worth and the impression we may make on others seem but small reward for the discipline and effort put forth.

Possibly it all boils down to the fact that we are getting older all the time and our years are limited. Our main life work has been done. Our field of acceptance in the world is narrowing. We are no longer serious contenders for position or fame. So what will we ever do with more formal education? The obituary columns in our newspapers fortify this doubt of using or profiting by additional study and the acquisition of more and better skills. We tend, now, to check the age of those who have died and find ever so many of them in our general age bracket. If we have studied the New Testament at all, we may remember the fate of one retired man who decided to take it easy: "I will say to my soul, Soul, you have ample goods laid up for many years; take your ease, eat, drink, be merry" (Luke 12:19). That seems reasonable. We think of "ample goods" as including our present educational attainments. And the end of that ancient example of a retired man goes even further to confirm our unwillingness to strive mentally: "This night your soul is required of you; and the things you have prepared, whose will they be?" (Luke 12:20).

Added to the other not-so-good things about venturing into new educational fields is the wisdom of the old proverb, "*You can't teach an old dog new tricks.*" We have acquired patterns of life and habits that now seem to us as familiar friends and we doubt that we can make any changes. We stop for a moment to analyze what we are doing and find that this interruption of our instinctive response confuses us hopelessly. For instance, if a man pauses in his shaving to ask, "Which side of my face do I shave first and which hand do I use?" he finds it difficult to go ahead with his shaving. Left to themselves his reflexes would have carried him through his morning ritual without hesitation. And if a woman stops to ask herself which stocking she puts on first, or questions some routine part of her makeup she will

Educational Opportunities

be as lost as the man. These are small illustrations of the scores of things that we do without real thought. They are the result of early learning and continuous practice.

These physical examples can be matched by our mental processes and our emotional responses. Our minds follow thought channels cut deep through the years. Our loves and hates and prejudices, our likes and dislikes, faithfully go down the familiar road they know. How are we to change at our age? And education means change. Always. Why try the impossible? We may think of the play, *My Fair Lady*, and remember what desperate efforts were required of the young woman whose teacher was determined to change her from a street waif into a grand lady. Her manner of walking and sitting and holding a tea cup had to be changed completely. And, hardest of all, her speech had to be transformed from gutter Cockney, to cultured aristocrat. To succeed in her learning, her mind had to be patterned to give her body orders to do the new things in the new way. Ah, but she succeeded. Then why not we? But she was *young!* Could the same teacher have succeeded with that girl's mother or grandmother? We are sure the answer is no. Who are we, then, to go out as antiquated Eliza or Ezra Doolittles to classes and books and expect to come back as changed persons?

There is no use in minimizing the rigidity of our body and mind, or pretending that we may exchange new things and new ways for the old at will, or that the person we are now will politely make room for a new person. Our hope is, however, in examples proving that this has been done. Samuel Johnson, an eighteenth-century Englishman of letters, taught himself Italian when past the age of seventy. Grandma Moses began her art career in her late seventies. History has many such illustrations to show that it is not completely impossible to acquire new skills in our older years. If others did it, are we ready to say that we are inferior in determination to them? We might remember, too, that the effort to learn new things and come to a richer understanding of life is, of itself, a "new trick" available to all of us.

Making the Best of It

To make the best of our educational challenge we must not try to brush aside in an overly optimistic attitude the difficulties that we have explored or we shall come to grief quite early. If we start out knowing that *the beginning is bound to be slow* we shall not expect too much too soon. We may have heard a puzzled person, after he or she had listened to an involved statement of a speaker, say, "Would you run that past me again?" This illustrates the start that we must make. We shall not find that we can take hold of an idea and comprehend it perfectly all of a sudden. We shall need to run many things past our minds again and again before we are satisfied that we understand them. The difference with us now as compared to earlier years is like the contrast between a camera with flash equipment and one without. A person who brings to a subdued scene a camera with flash equipment can get a sharp impression of his film immediately, but the person whose camera lacks flash equipment must put up a tripod and take a time exposure. The time exposure will give a film impression that is good even though the process takes longer. With our youth may have gone our quick, flash learning abilities. We must now rely on longer exposure to what we desire to learn.

Our start is going to be even slower if we have been away from systematic study for some years. If the routines of school or of constant practice have been left behind for long, we'll find it hard to get back into the groove. On the other hand, we may find that we have kept up a discipline in a few things which may give us some leverage now. Some older persons have an unbroken record of memorization and can memorize just as readily as when they were young. But most of us have not memorized a line of poetry or a paragraph of prose for a decade or more and will find it rather frustrating to make the mind remember what is found in books or experiments.

This slow start need not be completely discouraging if we are prepared to expect it and are willing for our new efforts and patterns to develop gradually. We may recall the instructions that came with new cars in the past advising a "warm-up" period for the engine before driving off. New cars now do not require this precaution because of improved methods of lubrication. The older cars, too, had to be driven five hundred miles or more at a moderate speed for a "break-in" period. New cars now come to us already broken in by factory procedures. We older people still need the warm-up and the breaking-in when we set forth on an educational journey. But this need not mean that our eventual performance will be in any way inferior.

Recognizing the likelihood for a slow start prepares us to allot more time to our project at first. According to the nature of what we have selected to do we must study more hours, read over the assigned portion of a book or text more times, and practice oftener than in years gone by. However, as we gain assurance and proficiency we may well be surprised at how our abilities take on new life.

One real advantage of beginning with care and with repetition is that our foundation for the new work will be solid. When we say of products that we buy, "They don't make them as they used to," we are referring to the time and care given to the workmanship. The speedy methods of production and packaging now result in many imperfect articles going out into the world. When more of the work was done by hand, the quality was better. The same is true of houses. Prefabricated sections combined with production line fittings often result in less solidly constructed buildings. This same result can be found in hurried learning. At least, our limitations give us the benefit of forcing us to take our time and be thorough about what we attempt. And the end result will be that much more satisfying.

However, average human beings that we are, we shall grow impatient with delays. In weaker moments we will say, "It just can't be done!" We must become stern with ourselves when we are on the verge of *making excuses for giving up.*

And we shall need to watch lest we dawdle and give ourselves too many "breaks" from the task that we have set for our hands or mind.

Quitting is an obvious temptation at any period of life when the going is rough. It is especially attractive as we get older and the penalties for walking away from the job are few or nonexistent. We can find scores of excuses why we should not stay at an exacting or demanding task. First, we might say that we had made a mistake in our choice of the course or subject or skill selected. Why not admit our stupidity and avoid wasting more precious time?

And there is the excuse that we call "consideration for others"! Why should we slow down a class or exasperate an instructor by our inability to keep up with the procession? Or, if we are pursuing the learning on our own, why pretend that we are smart enough to do this thing? Could we not be doing something for others in the time that is being frittered away?

Traced down to the real reason, our quitting is due to pure laziness as much as anything else. We get spoiled by the lessening demands of the later years and find it hard to compel ourselves to do anything that gets in the way of doing as we please.

Frequent breaks from discipline of studying are nearly as bad as the excuses for quitting. In fact, they are more insidious because we persuade ourselves that we are simply resting in order to go back and lick the problem! Our breaks might be more frequent at first in light of our discussion regarding not planning too ambitious a schedule at the beginning. It is best to start with shorter intervals of study or work as we launch into a new venture, and then increase gradually the time and effort we devote to it. We shall not, then, feel such a strong need for interrupting ourselves frequently.

Why do we like to get away from a project we have started? We need to be honest enough to recognize that giving up may be one of our habits. A young writer had to tackle this weakness in himself. He said that before he sat down at his typewriter he went around the room and arranged his equipment carefully. He laid out pencils, erasers, paper, and the like. He pinned to the wall clippings and quotations that he thought might be worked into his manuscript. When he finally had everything convenient and ready to go, it was time for lunch and not a single word was on paper! An older writer said that he grabbed up a handful of paper and his wife's ironing board and his typewriter and set up shop anywhere that was fairly quiet and got down to work immediately. The latter writer turned out several books while the former was never published.

And, last, we may make the best of our challenge by *seeing to it that our educational program is well-rounded*. Some older people have a cast of mind that permits them to enjoy specializing. Most of us have acquired many interests. We would find a program of learning slanted in one direction not so enticing as one that encompassed several of our concerns. When we were looking at recreation and noted some advantage in making ourselves master of one sport, we did not assume that we would never play anything else. A change of pace is of benefit in any area of life, including one's continuing education.

If, for instance, we decide to concentrate on music, we would tire of practicing the same piece months on end. Our teacher will know this, too, and will guide us in trying out various forms of composition by a number of composers. By investigating the history of the instrument we are using and by studying the biography of one or more masters of that instrument we shall find that the practicing comes easier.

And while we are learning to play the instrument, our reading could well explore the general history of the period when the great musicians lived and did their work.

If, like Samuel Johnson, we have determined to learn a language we might add to the monotonous mastery of nouns and verbs and conjugations a course in the literature and customs of the people whose native tongue we are studying.

Further, it is wise to keep active physically and not concentrate entirely on mental pursuits. And there should be at least one interest of a social nature. A muscle that is not used becomes deformed and useless. For instance, an arm tied to the side for weeks cannot be made to move readily when it is loosened. If we become so engrossed in the study of one particular thing that our other interests and potentialities atrophy and shrivel up by disuse, we shall find little joy in the achievement we hope to complete. We must make sure that any educational program we lay out for ourselves takes into consideration our many needs and interests.

A HEALTHY MIND

In a strange hotel room I awoke during the night and was seized by terror. I saw the figure of a man, dimly outlined by the light from a lamp shining through the window. This intruder appeared to be a tall person wearing a hat. I could not see the face. Slowly and quietly I reached above my head and felt for the switch of the bed light. Suddenly the room was illuminated and I saw the "man" that had caused my heart to pound and my nerves to tingle. The "man" was my own coat and hat which I had hung on a clothes tree in the corner!

This illustrates how easy it is for us to allow unfamiliar things and words to scare us unnecessarily. Even as we look at the word *psychology*, with its awesome imports, we may be frightened. But if we throw the light of understanding upon that word we shall find only ourselves. *Psyche* means soul or inner self. And under the heading of psychology we group certain things about ourselves: feeling, thinking, and willing. We feel and think and will at all points in life. But as we get older the process that induces feeling, thinking, and willing is affected by the accumulated years.

The Good

What could be psychologically good about getting old?

The very fact of being freed from our "life's work" brings with it a pleasant sense of *euphoria — a feeling of well-being and release*. With our associates, the "good guys," we have been engaged in a great tug of war trying to pull the "bad guys" of want, insecurity, ignorance, violence, and disease across the line of change to make things better for ourselves and our loved ones and for coming generations. Now a replacement has arrived for us and we are no longer needed on the tug rope. Whatever we could do we have done, and that part of life is behind us. The urgency of the eight-hour day in office, schoolroom, factory, field, or home no longer drives us. Without being considered truants, dropouts, or loafers we are entitled to new schedules of our own, and pursuits apart from what has been expected of us during long years of toil. What we have achieved in the world stands and no one can deny it. We may not have achieved worldwide fame, but in our way we have done our part. We have voyaged out and put our feet on some moon of endeavor and are now back home. The world has no right to expect us to make the arduous and risky trip again, nor will it.

This removal from the tension of the routine and the "must" brings a consciousness of freedom never enjoyed before — even in childhood. Our youthful boast of "living our own life" is never as fully realized as when we get old. Before this period of life, we are constantly subjected to directions, imperatives, and necessities. There is a career to build, a family to support, an education to complete, a conpetency to achieve, a warfare to fight. Now we may extricate ourselves from the turmoil and find out whether or not there are better paths and better ways. We begin to see our heritage and the ultimate meaning of things from new perspectives. No longer do we say, "When I have time I shall try something new, I will travel to a place I have often heard of but never seen, I will give thought to understanding the way of the world." No, we do not say this now because we have the time and we are free to take off in new directions to the limit of our health and resources.

One of the first of the new directions may be found in *the opportunity for communing with oneself*. As Walt Whitman put it,

"I loafe and invite my soul." [1]

Among the many things he discovered about himself was:

"I am an acme of things acomplished, and I an encloser of things to be." [2]

What exciting things will we find out about our real inner self?

Without doubt the self merits inspection and will

---
1. Walt Whitman, "Song of Myself," in *Leaves of Grass*.
2. *Ibid*.

reward the examiner. Likely the estimation and image we have had of ourself will prove unworthy of that doughty person who has sparked all we have accomplished in life so far. Honest introspection may well clear away from the undervalued self the many layers of doubt, misconception and criticism that we have wrapped around it through the years. Likely we will find the actual inner self better by far than we had thought it to be through the decades of our fierce struggle in the world.

Perhaps this can be illustrated from one of Charles Dickens' novels. As I remember the story, two brothers were engaged in the practice of law. They specialized in overseeing the affairs of orphans and widows. The younger of the two attorneys occupied the outer office and conferred with the clients when they came to make requests for extra money or for permission to do something apart from the ordinary. The younger man appeared to be sympathetic and understanding, but he always sent the petitioners away disappointed. He told them that he would gladly say Yes to their request, but that his older brother had the veto power and would never agree to anything so unusual! So well did the crafty lawyer instill fear in the hearts of the clients that they did not dare insist on seeing the other man. However, one day a determined person braced the worst and pushed his way into the inner office. There he confronted the one whose reputation was so frightening. And he found, instead of the monster he had expected, a gentle, reasonable little man who listened courteously and promptly granted the

A Healthy Mind

request. The brother in the outer office, of course, was the stingy, severe member of the firm! As we penetrate deeply toward the abode of the real self we are more than likely to find that that self has been given a bad name, and that he deserves to be known.

It would be difficult to overrate the new sense of confidence it is possible to attain by knowing ourselves for what we are. We shall cease to expect more of ourselves than we can produce. But we shall also discover areas in which we can expect more sturdiness and a worthier performance in tough spots than we might have thought possible.

The search for our real self can be helped by utilizing some of the extra time that is ours to *strengthen family ties*. As we get older we sense in a new way the broken ends of kinship. In the pressure of earlier years there was a tendency to narrow the circle of the family to the extent of the old rhyme:

> Me and my wife,
> My son John and his wife;
> Us four
> And no more.

Perhaps there have been times of financial and health crises when our concern extended little further than "Me and my wife" and, occasionally, it may have stopped at "Me." The opportunity of keeping in touch with the family in all its branches is available to us as we get older and as we search for ourselves. The tragedy of hearing from one another only at holidays and of seeing one another only at funerals can be changed.

In a way, our years of top-speed living and

performance may have dammed us off from those outside the immediate concerns of our day-by-day encounters. Too often, the family is outside that dam and shut off from us, wondering why we never look their way. With reason, sons and daughters will say, "I never really knew my father," or "I never could get close to my mother." And if this is true of the people within the home, what must it be for the sisters, brothers, aunts, uncles, cousins, nephews, nieces, grandchildren, grandparents, and in-laws?

Cultivating and strengthening family ties in our years of more leisure can prove to be an exciting occupation. An older person in a family can be, to use a specialized term, the *ombudsman* for the clan. He can be the one to hear the cries for help and understanding. He can be the mediator among his brothers. He can initiate communication and reunions.

The current commendable urge to "find myself" and to discover "who I am" can be realized to a great extent by getting to know the members of the family. Each member of the family is equivalent to one ingredient of the family recipe. Put together these many ingredients make up the total contribution of that particular family to the world at large. If each family in the world made its best contribution, the world would soon be a more orderly, loving place. One of the wastes of mankind is the dissipation of family resources.

At this point, we might well warn ouselves of the danger of having ideas for the family that we try to force upon the other members. (And this self-counsel refers to all directions that our activ-

A Healthy Mind

ities of later years may take.) We should try to remember what it meant to us in the prime of life when older people, meaning well, threw our schedule off balance by placing some obligation upon us. We may recall, also, how hard it was to refuse their requests and demands. The wonderful freedom that comes to us as we get older should be thought of as a gift for making life easier and simpler for our family. Of course we would never want to be like children who get under their parents' feet whining, "I have nothing to do. Play with me." The highest kind of freedom, and the kind that is ours now, is completely self-reliant and self-contained. In our new freedom we should not need to draw upon the assistance of younger people. Indeed if our freedom has anything of dependence in it we are enslaved to that extent and are not free.

Beyond the family, we shall find *time to cultivate friends*. In younger days we may have said, carelessly, "I wonder whatever happened to so-and-so. We used to see so much of each other." As we get older we can say this same thing seriously and plan to do something about it. We may be amazed to find a smoldering ember of friendship left in the hearts of many whom we have not seen or spoken to for years. That ember may be kindled into new flame by a letter, a phone call, or a visit. Both we and the friends will have much to offer each other because of the passage of years.

Happily, we need not limit ourselves to old friends. New friends may be made, especially among our contemporaries. Some of the new friends may come from among people who have always been available in our immediate haunts. Some will be from among strangers who have come on our horizon because of our changing occupations or locations. Some, too, may be found as they move into our neighborhood. The cultivation of friendships offers a sure way of pushing out our boundaries. We need this to avoid the limitations of a narrow sphere of contacts.

With our new freedom also comes the temptation to announce to ourselves and others: "I don't have to do anything now that I do not choose to do! I am so tired of being told that I must go to this, I must do that, I must read this, I must attend to that." To a certain extent this way of exercising freedom can be good, but carried too far it will restrict us until we feel free no longer. With a large and scattered number of friends, our interests and concerns range far afield. I write to a friend in England. His replies bring me a breath of another distant land. His manner of expression and choice of words keep me aware that my way of doing and saying things is not the only possible way. The pictures he sends open to me new channels of imagination. And each of his letters closes with an eager invitation to write and tell him about my "doings" and my family.

The Not So Good

Having found some of the psychological good of getting old, we ought, in honesty, to look at that which is psychologically not so good.

First of all, there are *fears* with which to contend. If we ask why fears are more prevalent as we

A Healthy Mind

get older we might think of the act of walking on ice. The schoolboy who comes to a stretch of icy pavement exults in his good fortune and slides along with pleasure. If he falls he does so with laughing abandon, and is not hurt. But, as we grow older, we begin to treat icy pavements with greater respect. We realize that we do not move as supplely as we did when young. We know from our own experience or the mishaps of others our age that a fall can result in serious injury. If we think of the events of life as being as precarious as an icy walk we shall understand why fear crops up. Whatever we are called upon to say or do has in it a peril that we refused to admit when younger. A question is always before us. Will we end the day having acquitted ourselves with a minimum of foolishness and mistakes, or will there remain for the night hours a gnawing sense that we have come off second- or third-best and are the worse for the wear and tear and, possibly, that we have pulled the pride or well-being of others down with us?

This thought of involving others is a definite fear in and of itself. We say, "I never want to be a burden to anyone." We think of illness and disability. We think of a future when our money may be insufficient for some emergency. We think of the possibility of a stroke or some similar occurrence that will make us incompetent to care for ourselves.

Possibly this fear of ill health is one of the greatest fears that come with age. In the excitement of younger years we do not have the time to notice little aches and pains and "symptoms" that may indicate acute or chronic disease. With more leisure we are apt to dwell longer on every twinge and abnormality of function. We check these bodily discomforts against the articles we read in magazines and conclude that we are sinking into one or another of the dire conditions described.

Other fears have to do with family matters, with our ability to drive safely on crowded highways, with a possible inadvertent repeating of something that we should hold in confidence (in fact, we fear more than we realize the trouble that our tongue can get us into). We have deep within us a fear of death or, at least, of dying, although we may boast about our "readiness" and that we have "lived our life" and ought not to be "cluttering the earth." A list of fears would fill a long page. Each person's list would be similar, for the most part, but would have some unique concerns. Past history or experience elicits particular fears just as the burning of applewood gives off one odor and the burning of oil another. Basically, however, we share common concerns.

There is no use in saying that fears are foolish and — away with them! They are not to be dismissed so lightly. Perhaps our best weapon against fear is to realize that it will be a constant companion and must be so accepted. We may strengthen ourselves by remembering that few of our fears ever are realized. They exist only in our imagination, much like alarming dreams from which we awaken unharmed. A psychiatrist counseled his patients to say something like this: "Well, here is that foolish fear again, and it has

A Healthy Mind

not hurt me yet."

Another not-so-good thing is our *sense of being different from what we once were*. There is a mighty temptation to dwell upon what we "used to be." Ah, in our younger days we were this and that, and could do great deeds, but now we are insignificant and could not stand the old pace or measure up to the old responsibilities even if we were given the opportunity.

We may watch the younger people who pass our house in the morning on their way to school or work and contrast their purposefulness and their exciting day with ourselves and our comparatively unstructured and aimless hours. We know, too, that these younger people may notice us occasionally and say to one another, "It must be sad to get old. What has that old fellow (or that old woman) got to live for?"

This difference is not only of our own imagining. It is pointed out to us by legislators, writers, reporters, and others. The law, especially in the tax department, makes certain provisions for the younger population and altered provisions for us. Silly terms such as "senior citizen, "golden age" people, "pensioners," and "leisure village set" are bestowed upon us. If we go to a hospital we are stopped at the Medicare desk and then assigned to the geriatric ward.

Preferential treatment accentuates the difference that we feel so acutely. Besides the tax advantages, some communities offer free transportation and hot meals. Adult school classes are free to those over sixty-five. Churches and neighborhood groups plan outings for their "retired friends." In brief, we are pitied and coddled.

The whole matter of our inner feelings is summed up by our memories of what was in contrast to our realization of what is. Just as a person who loses an arm, a leg, or an eye bemoans the fact that he moves through life a bit differently from the average person he meets, so we feel keenly that age has given us a mutilation that can never be removed.

To deal with this not-so-good difference we need to accept the fact that it has come to us as it came to our fathers and their fathers, and as it will come to the sprightliest youngster passing us on his way to school. We are not exceptions to what has been called "the way of all flesh." And the most unbecoming thing we can do is to pretend that this difference has not touched us and endeavor to dress, speak, and act as though we are immune to the years.

Indeed, this difference can be turned to good effect. We know secrets of life that the young have yet to fathom. We have a wisdom that comes only with age. We have an airplane view of life while the younger people are absorbed pedestrians seeing only the scenes along their narrow way.

Another not-so-good aspect of life as we get older is our more pronounced *sense of guilt* as we take a backward look along the path that we have traveled. In our heyday we "let the chips fall where they may" as we hewed our way through the forests of love and work and endless responsibilities. But now we become increasingly aware of where those chips have fallen.

What, for instance, have we done to our wife

or husband that may have conditioned his or her life for the worse? What unhappiness have we caused that well might have been avoided if we had been more careful and less selfish? How did we fail to keep fresh our first love? Where does the blame lie that communication broke down?

And, if we've had a family, we look at our children and see something of failure every time there is a difficulty in the life of a son or daughter. We recall occasions when we were cruel in our demands, when we were indifferent to their unspoken needs, when we went off on our own affairs at a time when they desperately needed a father or mother available.

Even our dealings on the job and with our neighbors and friends come up for inspection. We retain raw memories of what we did and said amiss. How could we have been so blind? Some there were whom we used or exploited and cast aside.

And regarding our lifework, how well did we do the job that was ours? Did we slight the task because we could get away with a shoddy performance? Did we stop at mediocrity when we might have been among the leaders and creators in our field of endeavor?

Personal sins which we excused and rationalized away rise up to haunt us. The old indulgence of saying, "One must sow his wild oats." "Everybody is doing it," "Someone failed me and I had to release my hostility somehow on someone," "I am only human," no longer satisfies. The stark fact of the shortcoming will not be softened by reasoning.

To live with this sense of guilt we must look

at the problem carefully. We are justified to admit
that we are not perfect, have never been perfect,
and that we share this imperfection with all men
and women. We have committed many sins, it is
true, but we have done many good things also.
And we must accept the fact that what has been
done cannot be made better by constantly dwelling
upon it and blaming ourselves to the point of
desperation. Our best release from the burden of
whatever we have done that was wrong is to be
the best kind of person we can be from this
day on. We must be honestly sorry for the faults
of our past, confess them to God and those we have
wronged, and accept their forgiveness. We should
never fall into the trap of blaming ourselves un-
duly. We must try to take into account the occasion and context of those deeds or words that
worry us now, as a writer of another generation
pointed out: "An old man recalling the foolish
actions, but having lost the power of realizing the
feelings of his youth may be very unjust to his
own past." [2]

If we are the kind of people who worry about
our wrongdoings, then it may be that we are
magnifying what was done or said. The great
sinner is the one who does not care what wrecks
are strewn across his past and who secretly gloats
over the selfish conquests and waywardness. The
very fact that we are guilt-conscious can be a good
sign that we are properly sensitive to our relationships with God and man.

Finally, we discover within us as we grow older

---

2. W. I. H. Lecky, *History of European Morals* (New York: D. Appleton & Co., 1871), Vol. I, p. 141.

A Healthy Mind

a *loss of confidence.* As younger people we may have had the assurance of success that was expressed by a roistering character in a play of Shakespeare:

> Why, then the world's mine oyster
> Which I with sword will open. [3]

As we grow older we do not have that confidence that everything is possible and that nothing can stand against us. Diffidence and distrust of our abilities come along to take the edge from new explorations and projects. "Can't" replaces "can" with great regularity.

This lack of confidence will be exhibited in our checking and rechecking what we do. Did I turn off the light? Better go and see. Did I turn off the faucets that I was using? Better go back and make sure. Did I lock the door?

And if we drive we are likely to review the trip afterward wondering if we missed a stop sign, if the light we went through was green, if we missed seeing a school bus, and so on.

Another manifestation of the lack of confidence will be in the planning of a trip or project, or making a purchase. Firm and prompt decision will elude us, and we shall be irritated by our inability to be quickly definite. From having been Yes and No people, we find ourselves too frequently *Maybe* people.

This lack of confidence will be further intensified during periods of convalescence from illness, particularly if the disability has been from heart or artery trouble or strokes. Perhaps some of us

---
3. William Shakespeare, "The Merry Wives of Windsor," Act II, Scene 2.

will never know this acute lack of confidence to the degree described until we do have major physical problems, but to a certain extent this not-so-good tendency comes on as we get older. What then?

We may find help by noting that one of our failings is that we no longer trust ourselves to act automatically. When younger we never gave a thought to leaving a faucet running. If we had turned it on in the first place, we would have been sure to turn it off after use. And the same with talking and walking and driving. We trusted ourselves to react without needing to give thought to what we were doing. As we get older we find a need to remember each thing done, even the minor thing. To overcome this to some extent we should exert ourselves to concentrate on what we are doing and hold ourselves to alertness as we move through the day.

Also, an occasional bit of carelessness on our part should not be taken as a sign of senility. If we will notice, teenagers are just as prone to forget things and allow their minds to go off on a tangent as we are. And even the best of people in their prime are guilty of slips of routine and behavior. Unhappily, younger people have a habit of blaming the few bits of carelessness on our part to our age. If we were twenty years younger they would not give a second thought to our forgetfulness.

Greater confidence can be acquired by refusing to put importance upon small things, and by refusing to make a mental review of what we have done or said. A rearview mirror is helpful to a degree, but the windshield that provides a view of the road ahead is of greater value.

Making the Best of It

So we have looked at the good and not so good of the psychological aspect of getting older. We cannot wish away the annoying things nor can we multiply the good, but we can settle down and make the best of what there is.

We might start out by saying, "*I am still I.*" I am not a different person from the boy or girl of my school days. I am not a different person from the young man or young woman who charged out to make the world his or her "oyster," and who was swept off his feet by love. I am not a different person from the man or woman of prime years who had to be taken into account in the affairs of a family, an occupation, a community, and a world. I am not a different person from the one who stepped away from a lifetime endeavor into "retirement." The person who began at my birth is the person I am. Age has not nor cannot change my identity.

This is a comforting thought because we are used to that person with whom we have lived and fought these many years. Habits, customs, ways of thinking and speaking, familiar reactions to situations have not changed drastically. We can depend upon that tried-and-true (even if imperfect) person as long as we live.

In this connection, perhaps, we should warn ourselves against saying, "I am not the man I used to be," or "I am not the woman I used to be." If we speak in terms of physical capabilities, that is one thing, but to speak of the actual inner self is another. We need to reaffirm constantly, "I am the same man I have always been," or "I am the same woman I have always been."

To justify our insistence that we are the same person is the fact that there are telltale marks about us psychologically as there are physically. We know how law enforcement officers depend upon the infallible sameness of a fingerprint. A culprit cannot deny that he was at the scene of a crime if his fingerprint has been found there. So our feeling and thought and willing carry through life an identity that will survive the ravages of the years and prove that we are continuing to function in our own unique way.

To illustrate, when Englishmen and their wives went from their native land to serve the Empire in India, Africa, or some other faraway place, they maintained their custom of dressing for dinner. Even though the location was strange, and sometimes savage, they endeavored to sit down to eat whatever there was to eat as men and women of good breeding, manners, and courtesy. Also teatime brought a cessation of labor until the time-honored ritual was observed. Although the years may exile us into a strange sort of land compared to our earlier life, we can hold to habits and values we have cherished along the way.

The worth of knowing that we are still ourselves is that whatever comes to us as we get older must conform to our basic makeup and identity. If we are kind, courageous, enthusiastic, thoughtful, ambitious, independent, outspoken sloppy, or whatever, all that comes to us must

A Healthy Mind

submit to our mold. A poet recognized this:

> My heart leaps up when I behold
>   A rainbow in the sky:
> So was it when my life began;
>   So is it now I am a man
> So be it when I shall grow old. [4]

Even in our forgetful times we may be sure that what we do will be along the lines of what we are. We shall be preserved by our identity from straying far afield from our long-accepted standards of behavior and worth. This knowledge should do much to temper the new fears that we find assailing us now.

Another consideration in making the best of the situation is that now is the time to *use the resources that we have been laying up*. We have an expression, "I will put this aside for a rainy day." Usually we are referring to money or other material things. But we have also laid aside (without being aware of what we were doing) intangibles for a "rainy day." And our later years become our rainy days. Therefore, we may now take from our resources what is needed for a triumphant period of life.

Most of the intangible resources are laid up in our treasure house of memory. When an older person taps this treasure others say that he or she is reminiscing — recalling from past experiences. Older people frequently annoy younger ones by subjecting them to oral reminiscing of the "good old days." (The good old days to us are the days (when we were young!) But we should promise

---

4. William Wordsworth, "My Heart Leaps Up When I Behold."

ourselves not to be guilty of too much public and vocal reminiscing of this kind. Among contemporaries who gladly share this pleasure of recall, and silently to ourselves, reminiscing can be of great value.

In the Old Testament story of David and the giant Goliath, David reminisces when he recalls that he had killed both lions and bears in the past. He took courage from this memory as he went out to fight the Philistine. (See 1 Samuel 17:34-37.) This is the kind of resource that we have laid up. When a difficulty, pain, or deprivation comes to us we can search our memories and come up with our own success story in earlier onslaughts and be better able to bear what must be borne. For example, many younger people approach a hospital experience with fear because they have never had to cope with hospitalization before. But we older people, with few exceptions, have had at least one hospitalization and if we are ordered in again can draw on the earlier experience to remind us of what we may expect. We lived through it before and likely will again.

Another resource available is our sense of what seems right, good, beautiful, and purposeful that we have gathered through our living, reading, and listening. These can make up the theme of whatever life composition engages us. To illustrate, in a great symphony such as Beethoven's *Fifth* the musical variations extend to great lengths of melody and dissonance. They rise to shrill heights and sink to caressing softness. But behind all, the major theme comes through to us and, at the last, that theme ends triumphantly.

Our reminiscence of what we have found to be the dominant theme of life can be our background to all the swirling, confusing, and changing circumstances to which we must submit as the years go on. That theme can be with us to the end.

Out of our resources, too, will come the great and hard-earned lesson of the transiency of some things and the permanence of others. All that we can pull out of memory will confirm the words spoken by a king in an old poem, "Even this shall pass away."[5] Pain, sorrow, hunger, guilt-feelings, and fears are temporary. We have experienced them plenty of times before and they passed away. On the other hand, some things of worth came to us and never left. From his experience, Paul, the great religious teacher of the first century, listed three things that came to him and stayed; "Faith, hope, love abide" (1 Corinthians 13:13). These may be among our permanent possessions also. From our resources we can draw on some qualities that have proven indestructible.

Capping our efforts to make the best of what psychological changes may affect us may be our determination to *continue active in every way open to us in our condition, and to insist on being a vital factor in the world*. The worst thing that could happen to us would be a supine slinking out of the contemporary scene — a living in the past and an indifference to all except what touches us immediately.

If after we have been faced with the disappointment and shock of change that come with getting older we decide to "retire" in earnest, and

---

5. Theodore Tilton, "All Things Shall Pass Away."

if we cringe before every blow or draw the covers of life over our heads, we are done for. We need to force our minds to cut new channels necessary to pass the blockage that age has brought to our thinking and feeling and willing processes. This must be done as resolutely as it is accomplished in the cardiac wards of some hospitals. There is a special little flight of stairs for the use of heart patients. After a massive heart attack the body must contrive ways of getting blood around the blockage to deliver it where it is needed. New passages must be opened. Unless the patient exerts himself and makes demands upon his heart, this new adaptation will not occur and the patient will die.

This, of course, is easier said than done, but do it we must. The noted preacher, Harry Emerson Fosdick, said in his autobiography, "At threescore-years-and-eighteen I find this generation the most stimulating, exciting, provocative — yes, promising — era I have ever seen or read about. I am not yet ready to die. I want to see what is going to happen next." [6] This is an example of an older man's continuing curiosity and activity. His feelings and thinking were working as hard as ever. It might well be assumed that this outlook on life had something to do with Dr. Fosdick's living to the age of ninety-one.

It comes down to deciding on what kind of punctuation to life we are willing to accept. If getting older to us means the end of our book of life with the rest of our years merely a postscript,

---

6. Harry Emerson Fosdick, *The Living of These Days* (New York: Harper & Bros., 1956), p. 319.

A Healthy Mind

then we must beware. But if we demand that it be known that we have simply ended another chapter and are starting immediately on a new chapter, we are on the road to a fulfilling and fruitful old age.

And the matter of being a vital factor in the world can be more than wishful thinking. The attitude taken by some, "I don't matter anymore, My work is done. I am of no consequence to anyone or anything," is deadly. The painter, Picasso, at the age of ninety was asked by his friend, the bullfighter Dominguin who was then forty-six, whether he would advise him to get back into the bullring. The answer of the aged artist was: "Luis Miguel, you can be killed by a bull but what more could you ask for? What more could I ask for than to drop dead while painting? When a man knows how to do something and fails to do it, he is no longer a man. This is why you, Luis Miguel, must return to the plaza and die in the most decorous way possible. It is your duty." [7]

Whatever we can do, under present conditions of health and opportunity, we should do — not only for our own benefit but for the good of others. We can think of ourselves as pieces of a puzzle, each with a shape not to be found in any other piece, and of the world as a giant jigsaw-type puzzle. Something will be missing and incomplete if we do not fill the spot designed for us. The will and the determination to be a factor in the world are of great importance to our inner being. We should want to be among those whose

---

7. *Newsweek*, October 25, 1971, p. 102.

thoughts and opinions and probable reactions are borne in mind by those who project changes in our community and country.

SPIRITUAL STRENGTH

Now we are in trouble!

Up to this chapter we have ventured boldly and have accepted the pronoun "we" because our explorations have found all of us on common ground. We have discussed the problems and hopes of the physical, social, financial, recreational, educational, and psychological aspects of getting older. Age has been seen as no respecter of persons, but it has touched us all. When age knocked on the door it did not ask who we were. Age simply proclaimed, "Whoever you are, here I come!" But now, when we realize that the six aspects of the older person cannot give a complete picture of the aging man or woman since there is a spiritual dimension to life, we wonder how we can go on together without losing our common concern?

There are, of course, basic general searchings of the inner person that strike a kindred note in us all. However, what validity the author has been able to achieve in the previous chapters has been due to his speaking from his own personal experience and observation. If the author is to continue to offer this same level of counsel in this chapter he must not deviate from his own spiritual experience and observation. He must not yield to the superficiality that would come of deserting his personal spiritual background. This is especially required since whatever strengths and fortifications he has found for his later years and which he feels are worthy of describing here, are grounded in the particular soil of his own spiritual pilgrimage — a pilgrimage of Christian commitment. Even so, any reader should find here starting points for his independent soul-searching.

As we begin our search for the spiritual foundation, we might remind ourselves that we have found, not to our surprise but to our regret, that the aging process is irreversible. Change and deterioration threaten us in every avenue that we have explored so far. Now we are ready to inquire, Is there the same irreversible change and the same creeping deterioration in the spiritual department of the older person? Strangely enough, we may well find that getting older touches the spiritual in such a way that growth and improvement can occur. We have had to admit that the self is housed in a vulnerable body controlled by a vulnerable mind, but this vulnerability does not extend to the indestructible "I" within.

Let us see if we can make good on this encouraging conclusion.

All Good

For the other areas of life we grouped our findings under The Good, The Not so Good, and Making the Best of It. In the spiritual area there can be but one category: All Good.

This goodness begins at the point of recognizing that *a faith that is strong enough to live by is a constant and invariable part of existence.* Our faith is like the north to which we align our compasses, our sundials, and our magnets. It is like that temperature called "zero" to which thermometers are scaled. It is like the standard of time (such as Greenwich) to which clocks and watches are set. Anything that represents to us our absolute of belief is that to which all else must be brought for setting and testing.

For those of us who accept God and immortality, two anchors steady us as we get older and look, with no little dismay, at the increasing number of leaks in our physical craft and become aware of our lessening ability to man the pumps and keep the ship afloat!

As we try to take a close look at this faith of ours, it is well that we be aware that faith is so intimate and personal that it is impossible for any two of us to have an identical spiritual understanding. If one of us could put his or her faith on top of the faith of anyone else it would be found that one faith jutted out beyond the other at some points and was crimped in others. No two expressions of faith will coincide point by point but the major portion of the two faiths will show an amazing similarity. It is more than likely that the juts and crimps of the faith outlines have resulted from our lifelong training and our years of following a particular religious tradition. As we get older we find the improvement of being able to concentrate on the central truths of the faith and to take less seriously the nonessential differences of names and forms and rituals and disciplines. The smaller things may well have been helps to fortify our faith as we were in the process of maturing and needed symbols and illustrations, but the closer we come to true maturity the less will be our need of these props. Our faith will be able to stand alone.

That part of our faith which embraces belief in a future life within the plan of God clinches our assurance of indestructibility, and brings a feeling of serenity even as we go downhill in other ways. In fact, this faith explains the aging process — it gives us a reason for getting older. Christmas, or some other major holy day or holiday, could never come if we insisted on holding on to the months preceding it. Time must be allowed to elapse. Also, the privileges of adulthood do not come by our remaining children. And the solution to a mystery story does not appear if we refuse to read beyond the middle of the book. It follows, then, that unless we get older we cannot enter into a better and eternal life. Or, to look at the situation from a different angle, no wrapped gift can be seen and enjoyed until the cardboard, paper, string, or ribbon are removed. So it is that our material wrappings must fall away before the never-ending "I" can be free to experience and become part of immortality.

If we are ready to accept the fact that our faith

is one possession that need not suffer from getting older, then we are ready to go down any road that will improve and strengthen that faith. One direction we may take is that of *trying to understand and mark out the differences in faith that we find as we communicate with others* of our own age. If we can attempt this without prejudice, we may be started on a real adventure which will help us and the others to single out the prime convictions that we hold in common.

Prior to our present state of maturity, we may have been all too ready to classify our neighbors, friends, and acquaintances as Protestant, Catholic, Baptist, Mennonite, Pentecostal and so on. But now we may look upon them as fellow wayfarers who have grown older along with us, and we may help our own faith by discussing with them their belief concerning God and a future life.

Of course, if we have isolated ourselves in this one area of life — the spiritual — up until now, a new resolution to share with others may be impeded by the old walls of separation. We may need to do some bulldozing to throw down life-long hesitancies and barriers of prejudice or shyness. But there will be the great reward of finding people with much the same searching about the permanent that stirs us. If we have a great reluctance to "open up" to others on matters of our faith we may be helped by the story of a timid boy. This lad felt impelled to confront another boy for some slight or indignity and he sought him out with some inward quaking. When he found his foe he was even more terrified. The boy stood behind a fence and appeared to be very tall. Driven, however, to do or die, the first boy went around the fence and found the other to be standing on a box. The two of them were of equal height! Perhaps we are simply imagining that others will overwhelm us if we speak of religion. Or it may be that we have climbed on a box of superiority in the spiritual realm and are frightening off others who need our affirmation of faith. As a matter of fact, aging is a great leveler of human need and we shall be amazed to find how much we have in common with others.

The skill of listening that we explored earlier will stand us in good stead now. If, after we tell others of our faith and hope in these later years, we are willing to listen to them there could be a great strengthening of faith for all — not a coming together into sameness, perhaps, and certainly not a compromise for politeness' sake, but a firming of individual faith for each. The old, automatic "brush-off" attitude toward one not of our church or place of meeting can give way to a tendency to hear what underlying convictions have made the other person the man or woman that we see now.

There may have been times when an eager witness of some faith came to our door asking us to look over some literature. Or a representative of a nearby parish might have appeared, card in hand, to take a religion census. Perhaps we dismissed these people abruptly with a feeling of annoyance. However, as we now are getting older, we come closer to the realization that all people are in "the same boat" with us in life, and earlier walls of separation and the intolerance toward confronting other views, seem less important

Spiritual Strength

than they did in our younger days. If, by God's grace, we feel that we have a sturdier and better grasp of eternal truth than some others, how are we to share what we have and strengthen them if we do not know their thinking? And if, by some unhappy chance, we do not have the best possible light on the deep things of life, how are others to help us unless we listen to them? The weight of these considerations comes upon us as we get older.

Further, this talking to others about our faith and theirs, our willingness to read something that seems of great importance to them and, perhaps, an occasional visit to their places of worship may make of our human situations something a bit nobler and more promising.

In our development of communication in the field of faith is the commonly shared sense of human brotherhood of all people. If, in our earlier years, we felt this brotherhood could not intrude past the moat dug around our spiritual life, and if this impediment encouraged intolerance and division, now in our later years is the time when all of this should be rethought. If we can bring ourselves to include the spiritual area in our feeling of brotherhood and look with kindliness and sympathy even upon those whom we may have classed as unbelievers, then we are on the way to seeing the similarity of our struggles, our fears, and our moments of courage.

Another shared conviction that will come to light is that, despite what the years have done to us, most of us have clung to the belief that there is an overarching purpose in life and in the world.

Usually, many years are required for the building up of experiences that confirm to us that events and labors are working out to an eventual good. As we compare with other older people concerning these things we shall be able to fortify one another.

A third common conviction that is almost bound to appear in comradeship in spiritual aspects of life is that most of us have become convinced that religious faith is likely to result in an ever-increasing value set on love. Even in the midst of a world in turmoil, a world made up of individuals so afraid of one another that they keep building up massive supplies of armaments and weapons, a world outwardly dedicated to self-preservation, we shall find in many older people a kindred desire to promote love and understanding.

A number of other shared convictions among the aging could be mentioned, but if we look at just one more we shall have listed those that are fairly representative. This last conviction is that older people take with some seriousness what our forefathers spoke of often as the "moving of Providence." By the time of our later years we have seen much, we have felt much that we cannot explain rationally. In strange combinations of happenings, and in strange and sudden bursts of joy within us we have felt the evidence of a loving and just power beyond our comprehension. Who among us who are older cannot recite and share at least one instance of having been brought out of some danger or trouble in a more-than-ordinary way?

With an open attitude and some curiosity toward

Spiritual Strength

the faith of others, we are ready to cultivate our own faith as never before. In fact, without a compassionate and understanding frame of mind toward the convictions of others it is impossible to enter into our own faith to the fullest extent. Jesus pointed this out in one of His teachings: "So if you are offering your gift at the altar, and there remember that your brother has something against you, leave your gift there before the altar and go; first be reconciled to your brother, and then come and offer your gift" (Matthew 5:23, 24). As older people we find that even though this is hard it is possible, and we shall find that our faith, therefore, becomes more satisfying to us and highly productive of good.

Another way to accelerate the cultivation of our faith will be *regular attendance* (insofar as our health and location will allow) *at the services of worship or meditation or fellowship available in our selected church or other place of gathering*. If our faith is to be the support needed in these older years, this attention to being with others should persuade us to reserve the time needed and to conserve our strength for it. Our weekly (or more frequent) experiences of worship should take easy preference over less important activities.

One of the real values of being in our place of worship is to lose ourselves and our mundane concerns in the atmosphere of God's presence. In our travels we may have entered a house with some awe after we had been told, "George Washington slept here"! In the heyday of New England's literary giants some tourists would walk out to the home of Emerson and stare at his woodpile, and walk to the home of Longfellow to touch his gatepost. In Russia seemingly endless lines of people go into the Kremlin to be near the tomb of Lenin. Within all of us is some trace of this desire to be where the great have been. Is it not natural, then, that when we are in a place devoted to worship we have a feeling of God's presence which will bless our being? It is possible for us to lose ourselves and to loose ourselves from burdens in quiet contemplation and mind-searching in such a situation.

Added to the absorption of entering into our own kind of communion with the unseen, and the encouragement of being with others who share out aspirations, there is the opportunity for active participation in the ritual or service. Usually this participation is a sharing experience with all who have gathered. Our voices join with the voices of others whose faith has the same foundation as ours. Faith is a lonely affair in essence, but also faith puts down new roots each time it is expressed in company with people of similar convictions. Faith is recharged and kept in the best possible repair when brought to joint concerns of the Spirit. Have we not often read a book or listened to a speech which brought from us the glad remark, "That's exactly how I feel about that subject!" If the book had not been written or the speech made we would have held to our opinion without their assistance, but to know that another is of our mind is bound to bring reassurance.

Not only is there profit just in being in our place of worship sharing vocal expression with others, but there is the extra opportunity for strengthening and enlarging faith by assuming a share of the outreach suggested by the worship experience. Places of worship are not provided automatically or kept in good condition miraculously. The outward events of worship depend upon people. Certain of these responsibilities that are not too difficult for us who are older may include the giving of time to serve on boards and committees, and to accept special teaching assignments. Of course, we may find that the younger people rarely consider us for the "key" spots, but what of that? We have had our day and now even the smaller posts can be important to us and to the cause we serve. Let others be chairpersons and moderators. We have experience and acquired wisdom to bring to discussions.

A further compulsion growing out of our profit from our worship experiences will be the desire to extend the good things of our faith to those who may not have come to a way of spiritual maturity. Any group of people organized around the Christian faith, for example, will be impelled by that faith to take note of the great needs of the world in all areas of life and respond in compassion and with constructive projects. Taking our part in what our faith prompts our group to do for the hungry and oppressed, as well as for the spiritually confused, will be good for the ones we seek to serve and will be good for us.

When away from the place of worship, we have another method of cultivating our faith, and that is by *spending some of our additional time with our Bible — our Holy Book*. Faith, especially in our older years, must have a positiveness if it is to sustain us. This conviction need not result in intolerance, but in a serene, personal confidence. The important thing about much reading of our Bible is that we may grow in our understanding of why we believe that we have the best of all possible faiths. And, of course, we ought to be ready to accept from our Bible corrections of any wrong assumptions that we have allowed to gather in our system of belief.

This reading of our Bible must not be like that of a boy who promised his mother that he would read at least one chapter of the Bible each day. Frequently he came to bedtime without having kept his promise and he would turn quickly to the Bible, leaf through it hastily until he found a short chapter, and read as few verses as possible to fulfill his vow. In a short time this boy became an expert on the contents of the briefest chapters in the Bible! This kind of reading is childish and not for our older years. We need to set a goal of greater apprehension and understanding. This can be reached only by planned and methodical reading. Even if our daily portion cannot be too long it can be part of a directed and consistent schedule. Our reading will help strengthen our faith and clear away the debris that we may have gathered through the years because we took without question what others told us we should believe. We can provide ourselves with ammunition to use when anyone asks us, "Why do you say that about religion? Why do you go to that church?" If we know the answers to our own satisfaction nothing else can be required of us.

For those of us with reasonably good eyesight and with the inquiring cast of mind, reading some religious books from various traditions can broaden our understanding. Dipping into these books will not make converts of us, but it will bring us to a better understanding of others whose beliefs differ from ours. If we hope, as older people, to live with others in the best spirit of comradeship we need to understand their spiritual strivings even as we hope they will understand ours. Sometimes we may say, or hear others say, "Let's talk about anything except religion. That's a touchy subject, and we might step on some toes." But doesn't this mean shutting others out of the best part of our lives, and doesn't it shut us out from the best part of theirs?

As an illustration, an American missionary had been teaching in an African village for several years and then came home on a furlough. He wanted to send back to the village a gift that would be useful and beautiful. He finally chose a sundial and had it shipped. When the villagers opened the box and saw what they had received, they admired the fine finish and polish of the metal. In fear of having the lovely present damaged by the weather, they built a little hut over it so that no rain or sun could touch it. When the missionary returned to his job the people proudly took him to the little hut and showed him how carefully they had protected the sundial! This could be our mistake if we refuse to discuss our faith with others and refuse to look at their faith. A sundial or a faith cannot serve us without being exposed to the light of life.

Going back to our Bible, how much has our day-by-day living really been guided by its teachings? Occasionally, polls are taken to find out how much Christians know about their Book. And, if we can trust the published results, the knowledge of the average man or woman is deplorably low. This is tragic at any age, but it can be disastrous for us who are getting older. We can learn some things apart from our Bible by watching and copying others in their words and manner of life, but genuine faith is something that must have a personal quality independent of all others. Doctors may improve their skill by watching and listening to other physicians, but they must read the standard books in the medical field and come to their own conclusions if they hope to be able practitioners. Lawyers must be familiar with the basic works on law. Teachers search out background books on teaching techniques and the teaching experience of the ages. These three professions touch mankind in a critical way and all who dare to be among the ones to do this touching must know for and of themselves what it is to heal the hurts of people. What is vitally true for these professions is true of the most vital and vulnerable area of our later years — our faith. Faith touches us and through us all with whom we live and share the world. We need to know the Bible from firsthand study.

Through the Bible we believe that God has revealed to us a way of life that can lead us successfully from youth to age and beyond. And in the Bible we have what we might call clinical case studies of people no more gifted or better than we who lived by faith or went against it. We may observe the route of those who went before us and note what happened to them.

In the Bible are examples and directions for prayer and worship. If we seek to find an age-old answer to the age-old question, "What does God require of me?" we find the answer as we read. Indeed, our thoughtful and regular reading of the Bible can show us how to face up to the demands of life in a triumphant way. The haunting questions about suffering and death are dealt with in an understandable way.

As we grow older we shall find a number of ways to deepen the inner life, but one of the best for Christians is an inquisitive exploration of the Bible.

Continuing our efforts to achieve a rich, spiritual maturity, we may find that *an adjustable program of giving* and helping will round out the tangible opportunities. The program needs to be adjustable inasmuch as our financial obligations and the state of our health will vary over the months and years. Any program set up that becomes rigid and exacting could well be a source of guilt feelings and frustrations at each breach of our contract with ourselves. This would surely defeat its purpose.

The matter of giving should involve money, time, and a share of our skills and experience. We can grow spiritually if there is enough of an outflow from us to keep a freshness within. Age or retirement, or both, cannot justify a Dead Sea sort of existence where we take and keep insisting that our days of giving are over. Stagnation is just as possible and deadly to the inner person now as when we were younger.

To look more closely at a program for giving money — how much of our limited income should be made available to help alleviate the want and needs of less fortunate people? How much should be entrusted to our church or other organizations for the purpose of spreading our faith with all its richness? The conclusions to the earlier chapter on finances suggests some guidelines for personal, family, and community responsibilities that must be discharged before we can assess the amount available for free use. Inasmuch as most of us have a fixed income, with little chance of a windfall, we can be fairly definite in arriving at a sum for giving. Only a certain amount will be available for such use, and we must decide how much of that we need to contribute in order to satisfy our urge to be of help in the world. What we give must approach a sacrificial level if it is to touch our need for spiritual growth. Giving to causes of compassion or mission only what we have left after we have provided handsomely for ourselves brings no advancement of the spirit.

Perhaps our most precious possession available for giving — even ahead of money — is time. What hours or days will we give in service to people? Earlier we looked at the volunteer services that cry out for personnel. Now we relate these opportunities to our spiritual maturity. Devoting ourselves to some useful project at certain periods of the week, or to several projects, will give an immense lift to the inner person. Since time is so precious to us now, we are really giving of ourselves when we spend some of it unselfishly in acts of mercy and love. This is particularly true when we accept obligations at the expense of something we would rather be doing with the hours involved.

Added to giving of money and time is the opportunity of sharing the skills and experience we have developed during our lifetime. It is one thing to set aside the burdens of a job or profession after thirty-five years or so, and another thing to say to the world, "You have no right to expect anything more from me in that field — ever again!" Our desire for a complete change of occupation is understandable and, at first thought, seems to be right and wise. But are we willing to waste all of the ability and knowledge that have come to us slowly and painfully through the years? Would a retired medical doctor, for instance, feel content to walk around a victim of a street accident and go on his way saying to himself, "I have worked at healing for so long. Now I'm retired"? And why should any of us react differently than that doctor if we find a situation that calls for what we know and can do? As an example of using skills, the Peace Corps and Vista programs of the government urge men and women of mature years to volunteer to do things they know best how to do in places where other skilled persons are not available. Many opportunities not tied in with such ambitious programs will come along, and we will need to decide whether or not we are willing to give of what we have.

In whatever program of giving and helping we determine to follow, we may well find it wise to set aside some of our money, time, and talents for the spontaneous and emergency calls that are bound to come. Earthquakes, fires, famines, and other natural disasters destroy people's homes and resources. How wonderful to have reserved something to send off immediately, or to be on the spot helping in these crises! As an illustration, some time ago the newspapers carried the story of a blind man who hoped to see again. He had saved up several hundred dollars for an eye operation and had secured an appointment with a surgeon and a reservation in a hospital. But someone heard of the savings and broke into his house and stole the money. When his plight was made known publicly, this man received contributions from several people who had put money aside for such events. The surgeon promised to give his time without charge. Two people volunteered to transport him to the hospital. Many similar emergencies will come to our attention in our communities, our country, and the world at large. A bit of leeway in giving, and budgeting our time on a regular basis, will enable us to be among those who step forward in times of direct need.

We have surveyed some of the tangible expressions of growing into spiritual maturity. We may have sensed that underneath all of these strivings has been a deep motivating factor. To get at this motivating mystery, we might look again at the life areas which we have covered in this book by chapters.

We have found that the physical, social, financial, recreational, educational, and psychological represent somewhat distinct sections of our life. We might think of each as a spoke in the wheel of life. But can we think of the "spiritual" as just another of the several spokes? In our younger days we may have had this impression to some extent. Sunday, perhaps, was set off as a day for dealing with the spiritual. Even though a certain part of each day might have been set off for devotional reading and prayer, that part was somehow unrelated to the real business of Monday through Friday. A departmental mode of living seemed natural and workable. But as we got older, we began to sense a binding force in all of life's activities that holds everything together.

This spiritual part of life provides the rim into which all spokes are set. It makes possible a smooth, forward motion. This rim touches all of the six areas of life with the same firmness and dependability. Even if we try to stress one area of life above all others — such as the financial — the spiritual will not accept that section as more blessed than any other. All of the spokes are of value to keep life moving without jolts and lopsidedness.

The spiritual rim of life ensures wholeness. No spoke, section, or area can extend beyond the rim. We are saved from abnormalities of behavior and may achieve a good life balance if we have this spiritual control. Until Scrooge (in Dickens' *Christmas Carol*) provided his life with a spiritual rim, he could not resist making financial affairs the ruling part of his life. As we get older, we begin to take more notice of this spiritual dimension and realize more fully that nothing in life can be complete or beautiful in symmetry that does not come within the spiritual frame.

Another advantage to having a sturdy spiritual rim is that we shall make a track on the surface of life to indicate that we have passed by — a trail for others to follow. Indeed, it is only by the spiritual part of life that our total person can make a lasting contribution to the world.

The more we permit the spiritual aspect of our life to invade and shape our other dreams and actions, the more we shall come to a state of peace and serenity that nothing else is able to bring. Throughout the years we have been trying to answer the How, the Where, the When, and the What of life's efforts and strivings. Now God gives us the all-embracing answer of the Why. And until we have this answer of the Why we cannot say that we have matured, no matter how the years pile up. Why are we here? Why do we suffer? Why do we feel the urge to accomplish something lasting and worthwhile? Why are we to die? Without a satisfactory answer to these questions we cannot settle down to a rich and rewarding period of life and enjoy the fruits of our earlier labors.

This all-inclusive answer comes most clearly to the author through the teachings of Jesus as found in the New Testament. With authority He explains our yesterdays, interprets our today, and offers us a sure path to a blessed forever. Convinced of this we can agree with the poet when he said of age, "The best is yet to be." [1]

---

1. Robert Browning, "Rabbi Ben Ezra."

TOP OF THE MOUNTAIN

The slope to be climbed is climbed,
The upward struggle is past;
The growing pains are stilled;
The mined treasure is garnered.

Now, on top of the mountain,
For the moment aimless,
The retired person stands.
What is left to do?

Chattering he may boast of height achieved,
Of how fiercely he strove,
What agonies he suffered,
Sum up the possessions at his feet.

Or, he may turn to find,
Not an effortless slide down the other side,
But a slender stairway
Inviting to heights of the Spirit.

—— *Glenn H. Asquith*

GLENN H. ASQUITH has enjoyed a varied professional career. He has had experience as a businessman, instructor in college, parish minister, ecclesiastical administrator and editor, director of writers' conferences, and author.

His undergraduate work was done at Eastern Baptist College and Seminary, and his continuing education courses have been in the field of pastoral counseling. His seminary awarded him a Doctor of Divinity degree in 1952.

He is particularly well equipped to address older people. He was a planning member of the New York State Conference on the Aging in 1955, a member of the White House Conference on the Aging in 1961, and more recently has been involved in the current American Baptist project, "Alternatives for the Aging."

Two of his books are made up of inspirational reading for older people and were published by

Abingdon Press in larger-than-average type: *Lively May I Walk* and *The Person I Am*.

As he says, "Who knows more about the dreams and limitations of the older person than one who has, himself, reached the state of retirement and the age of 70!"